W9-CXT-563

BELIEF, CHANGE AND FORMS OF LIFE

BELIEF, CHANGE AND FORMS OF LIFE

D. Z. Phillips

HUMANITIES PRESS INTERNATIONAL, INC.
ATLANTIC HIGHLANDS, NJ

BL
51
.P515
1986

First published in 1986 in the United States of America by
Humanities Press International, Inc., Atlantic Highlands, NJ 07716

© D. Z. Phillips 1986

Library of Congress Cataloging-in-Publication Data
Phillips, D. Z. (Dewi Zephaniah)
Belief, change, and forms of life.
Bibliography: p.
Includes index.
1. Religion—Philosophy. I. Title.
BL51.P515 1986 200'.1 85–27080
ISBN 0–391–03385–9

All rights reserved. No reproduction, copy or transmission of this publication may be made without written permission.

Printed in Hong Kong

To
Rush Rhees

Contents

Preface

With the present book, a certain cycle has been completed in my work. In *The Concept of Prayer*, I first began to urge that, in order to explore the grammar of the Reality of God, we should look to the contexts of prayer and worship. Unsurprisingly, most of the discussions of this essay since 1965 have concentrated on what they take to be its epistemological presuppositions. Very little attention has been paid to the analyses of the prayers, despite the fact that the whole burden of the book was to show that epistemological considerations cannot be divorced from such contexts.

In *Death and Immortality*, I tried to provide conceptual reminders of contexts in which the notion of the immortality of the soul has its home. I emphasised the essential differences between talk of eternity and talk of duration.

In providing conceptual reminders, a philosopher must also be aware of the reactions of his critics, and of differing philosophical developments in contemporary philosophy. In the essays in *Faith and Philosophical Enquiry* and *Athronyddu Am Grefydd*, I tried to come to terms with such criticisms and developments.

Religion Without Explanation marked a change of direction. I turned from contemporary philosophy of religion to examine influential attempts in early anthropology, sociology and psychoanalysis to explain religion away. Their efforts turned out to be misconceived even in terms of the methodologies of their own disciplines. In that book, I also explored Wittgenstein's discussion in *On Certainty* of Moore's truisms. I suggested that there are close parallels between Wittgenstein's treatment of fundamental propositions which are held fast by all that surrounds them, and the way in which the fundamental beliefs of religion should be discussed.

Yet, if fundamental beliefs in religion too are held fast by all that surrounds them, what happens when what surrounds them changes? It is evident that the meaningfulness of religion has been challenged in a host of different ways. In *Dramau Gwenlyn Parry*, a discussion of the work of a contemporary Welsh dramatist, and in *Through a Darkening Glass*, I was concerned, in the main, with the various ways in which religion and other ways of thinking may lose their hold on us. The possibilities of meaning and loss of meaning in religion are also one of my major concerns in the present essay.

It is highly probable that many philosophers will approach *Belief, Change and Forms of Life* armed with certain philosophical assumptions about the mode of argument they expect to find in the essay. This is because there are widespread philosophical theses concerning views which philosophers of religion influenced by Wittgenstein are supposed to hold. Over and over again it is said that these philosophers discuss religion as though it were an esoteric game, logically cut off from other features of human life. This game, according to the critics, is said to be understood only by those who play it, since the players themselves determine what does and what does not make sense in relation to it. According to the critics, it is said that the game cannot be criticised from the outside, and cannot be affected by any possible changes in personal, social or cultural life. No advance can be made to more substantive matters until these theses are refuted, since, surprising though it may seem, little effort has been expended to check whether anyone has ever held such views. That is why it has been necessary to begin the essay by showing that, so far from holding any of the theses which others have so confidently attributed to me, I have actually argued *against* every one of them!

Textual refutations in face of persistent misunderstandings, however, are no more than a preliminary step. The persistence of the misunderstandings itself needs explaining. It is important to see how Wittgenstein's own terminology concerning language-games has misled philosophers, tempting them to frame the unfounded theses I have referred to. Rightly understood, however, nothing Wittgenstein says rules out the possibilities of dialogue, understanding, criticism, change or decline where religious beliefs are concerned. Confusion may or may not be present in religious practices. Wittgenstein considers examples piecemeal; he does not indulge in *a priori* theorising. He rescues us from misleading tendencies of thought by the rearrangement of what we know when not philosophising.

So far, we have done enough, but no more than enough, to answer the often repeated criticisms of Wittgenstein's influence on the philosophy of religion. But further complexities must be faced. Wittgenstein's philosophical methods are relatively straightforward when what he discusses in rescuing us from our misunderstandings is the language we use when not philosophising. What happens, however, when the discussion of the language 'we' use is one of a use of language in which we do not participate? Here, Wittgenstein's methods would involve discussion of uses, possibilities of meaning, which, perhaps, we have never recognised, or which perhaps we have distorted by imposing alien criteria of meaningfulness on them. Such discussions are sorely needed in contemporary philosophy of religion.

When religious possibilities of meaning are threatened in a culture, some may take it upon themselves to remind the age in which they live of the possibilities it is growing away from. This can only be done when there are resources available to do so. Such resources cannot be taken for granted. Where they are absent, it may not be possible to provide religious reminders in a straightforward way. Nevertheless, in such situations, the task of philosophy remains unchanged: as always, it has to endeavour to understand what lies before it. 'Leaving everything where it is', not adding anything to it, involves giving an account of cultural turbulence as much as it involves giving an account of cultural stability. Charges of anti-intellectualism and conservatism against Wittgenstein in this context are entirely misplaced.

Further complexities have to be faced. Not only may philosophy fail to give an account of religious belief in the midst of its change or decline, philosophy may itself be one of the agents of this change and decline.[1] Philosophical theories often impose their own inventions on us and by doing so obscure the very phenomena we are trying to understand. The philosophical inventions may actually replace the meanings available to us before we started philosophising. It has been said that theology was invented in order to prevent people from thinking about religion. The same may be thought about the philosophy of religion from time to time. Instead of treating the world seriously, it creates systems of thought the effect of which is to make such treatment impossible. For example, the construction of tired theodicies obscures the ways in which the evils in the world present difficulties, problems and obstacles for religious belief. It is no surprise, as a result, to find religion accused of a failure to take the realities of human life seriously. Under the influence of such theodicies, religious belief may itself become something substantively different from what it could otherwise be.

The fate of religion is unavoidably determined by what happens to it in the complex relations of influences and counter-influences. Certain prevailing conceptions of philosophy of religion can give no account of these complexities. This is the case with externalism, the view that religious belief is answerable to universal criteria of intelligibility; and with internalism, the view that whatever is called religious is self-authenticating. But the facts and possibilities of cultural change must be taken seriously. When this happens, certain comforting religious pictures have to be abandoned. Believers cannot take comfort in the view that no matter what happens around them, the believer's heart is a secret place which cannot be affected by these events. They cannot argue that reason makes religious truths secure in a way that transcends all the possibilities of cultural change. Believers cannot assume that, no matter what cultural changes occur, religion can always accommodate them without loss of meaning or character.

Faced with threats to the intelligibility or even the existence of religion, its apologists may entertain the illusion that if only the right planning policies could be discovered, the future could somehow be *made* safe for religion. Movements, religious or otherwise, do not flourish by making their flourishing an aim. With respect to the future of religion, philosophy should not indulge in *a priori* optimism or in *a priori* pessimism.

Some apologists are reluctant to recognise the precarious character of religious belief. They argue, wrongly, that unless the future of religious belief can be shown to be *necessarily* secure, the beliefs in question could no longer claim to express eternal truths. The theologian, of course, will be concerned with what he takes to be the eternal truths of his religion. He will be alive to the task of having to elucidate and proclaim them for his age. He will also be alive to the diverse influences which threaten to distort these truths. The philosopher, in his turn, will be concerned to understand the theologian's situation, together with the tasks and dangers which confront him. Nevertheless, there will always be an essential difference between the philosopher's concerns and those of the theologian. Unlike the theologian, the philosopher is not the servant of the Faith. At times, however, a philosopher, and those who look to him, may grow impatient in wanting philosophy to play a more positive role. Philosophers of religion often write and speak as if *they* could provide remedies for the troubles facing religion in the midst of cultural change. In short, they begin to long for the emergence of a Christian philosophy. This hope is not only futile; it is one which corrupts the spirit of philosophical enquiry.

In this preface, I have given some indication of the course my enquiries take in this essay. It could be said that my central concern is with Wittgenstein's remark, 'to imagine a language is to imagine a form of life'. The essay's aim is to think of the varied implications of this remark when applied to religion; to see that it is difficult to overestimate the importance of saying that to imagine a religion is to imagine it in a form of life.

Acknowledgements

In this book, previously published papers have been reorganised and, in some cases, rewritten. The book also contains new material.

Chapters 1, 3 and 5 make use of material from a paper, 'Belief, Change and Forms of Life' which was delivered at a University of Notre Dame colloquium on Religion and the Notion of a Form of Life, held in March 1979. The paper was published in *The Autonomy of Religious Belief,* Frederick Crosson (ed.) (University of Notre Dame Press, 1981). Chapter 1 also uses material from 'Dylanwad Wittgenstein ar Athroniaeth Crefydd' (Wittgenstein's Influence on the Philosophy of Religion) which appeared in *Efrydiau Athronyddol* (1979). Chapter 3 also makes use of a small part of 'Alienation and the Sociologising of Meaning', a paper read at the Joint Session of the Aristotelian Society and the Mind Association at the University of Sheffield in a symposium with Anthony Manser, and published in *Proceedings of the Aristotelian Society*, supp. vol. LIII (1979). This material has been substantially rearranged and has many additions. In all three chapters, new material has been included and some significant changes have been made to the original papers.

Chapter 2 is made up, in the main, of the paper, 'Wittgenstein's Full Stop', delivered at the University of Western Ontario in a colloquium to mark the twenty-fifth anniversary of Wittgenstein's death. It has been published in *Perspectives on the Philosophy of Wittgenstein*, Irving Block (ed.) (Basil Blackwell, 1981). New material has been added, and there has been some rearrangement of the original material.

Chapter 4 consists largely of the paper, 'The Problem of Evil' and its 'Postscript' presented at a Royal Institute of

Philosophy Conference on the philosophy of religion at the University of Lancaster in a symposium with Richard Swinburne. 'Postscript' took account of Swinburne's criticisms of my paper and also of the criticisms of John Hick who chaired the symposium. Paper and postscript were published in Stuart C. Brown (ed.), *Reason and Religion* (Ithaca and London: Cornell University Press, 1977). In the present essay, some new material has been added, and there have been changes in the presentation of the original material.

Chapter 6 makes use of a small part of the paper, 'Belief, Change and Forms of Life' already referred to. In the main, however, the chapter makes use of a paper, 'Can There Be a Christian Philosophy?' written during a second visit to the Perkins School of Theology at the Southern Methodist University, Dallas, in April 1979. It was a response to Charles M. Wood's paper, 'The Aim of Christian Theology', *Perkins Journal*, vol. XXXI, Spring 1978. It was published in *Perkins Journal*, vol. XXXII, Summer 1979, which has a response from Charles M. Wood.

I acknowledge all concerned with gratitude for permission to make use of this material in this essay.

I am extremely grateful for the detailed work on the manuscript by Margaret Leach. I am also grateful to Donald Evans for reading the earlier versions of the present essay, for his valuable suggestions, and for his help in proof-reading. Once again I have been extremely fortunate in benefiting from the excellent preparation of the typescript by Mrs Valerie Gabe, Secretary to the Department of Philosophy.

Department of Philosophy D. Z. P.
University College of Swansea

1 Wittgenstein and Religion: Fashionable Criticisms

It may be that Wittgenstein's influence on the philosophy of religion has aroused more hostility than any other aspect of his work. The years since the Second World War have been described as 'a sorry time for the philosophy of religion in English-speaking countries', and this, it is said, has been due not least to the disastrous influence of Wittgenstein.[1] During the period referred to, the influence of Wittgenstein has been far-reaching in almost every branch of philosophy: philosophical logic, philosophy of mathematics, theory of knowledge, philosophy of mind, ethics, aesthetics, philosophy of the social sciences, and so on. Adverse comments on his influence on the philosophy of religion, however, are not confined to those who think that Wittgenstein's philosophical influence in general has been a disaster. On the contrary, they are made, as in the instance quoted, by sympathetic commentators. Unfortunately, it cannot be denied that a philosophy by innuendo has grown up by which it is hinted, rather than argued, that what Wittgenstein is said to have said about religion and ritual is not closely related to the rest of his work. It has been suggested also that those influenced by him in the philosophy of religion have imposed alien features on Wittgenstein's work, and made use of certain of his terms, such as 'language-games', in ways of which he would not have approved.

It is hard to see how these charges can be sustained. If we look at some other areas of philosophy, we shall find a continuity between many of Wittgenstein's emphases there and those we find in his comments on religion and ritual. For example, logic, for Wittgenstein, is not an *a priori* realm which is, in some sense or other, prior to all experience. Distinctions between sense and nonsense have their life in activities and ways of living we share with one another. We see their force, not by reference to external, static standards, but by appreciating the different bearings things have on one another. In epistemology, Wittgenstein attacks the search for foundations. Our task, in face of scepticism, is not to show *how* we know, or to ask *whether* we know. Rather we are asked to reflect on the tendencies of thought which lead us to ask such questions. When these routes to our questions are revealed, we cease to be in the grip of scepticism. In the philosophy of mind, Wittgenstein argues that we do not need theories to provide us with foundations for human behaviour. When such theories are abandoned – various forms of mind-body dualism, various forms of behaviourism, various forms of physicalism – they can be shown to harbour conceptual confusions. But what is offered in replacement? Not an alternative theory, but release from those knots in the understanding which had led us to general theorising in the first place. In ethics and aesthetics, the idea that philosophy should provide foundations or justifications for moral or aesthetic excellence is an example of the 'chatter' Wittgenstein said he wanted to put an end to in these contexts. Attempts at ignoring the heterogeneity of the moral and the aesthetic only lead to the construction of spurious unities. It has been observed that the variety in these contexts is important, not in order that we might fix our gaze on the unadulterated form, but to keep us from looking for it.[2] The search for essences in the philosophy of the social sciences, the desire to determine the essence of the difference between what is rational and what is irrational, has led to condescending misunderstandings of certain activities in our own culture and, more particularly, to condescending misunderstandings of activities in the cultures of other peoples. By ignoring the concepts which characterised these activities, alien descriptions were imposed upon them.

We find, then, in all these areas of philosophy, a refusal to make philosophy the provider of foundations and justifications. Yet it is this very refusal which is resisted when philosophers turn to the philosophy of religion (and, interestingly, political philosophy). But here, too, the same emphases can be found in Wittgenstein's work. He refuses to look for proofs for the existence of God. He refuses to look for philosophical foundations and justifications for religious belief. Here, too, the task of philosophy is descriptive. Elsewhere, Kenny recognises that this conception of philosophy is at work in Wittgenstein's discussions of religious belief: 'In saying that in philosophy there are no deductions Wittgenstein set himself against the type of philosophy which offers proofs, e.g. of the existence of God or immortality of the soul . . . . Throughout his life he remained sceptical and hostile to philosophy of that kind. "We must do away with all explanation," he wrote, "and description alone must take its place." The point of the description is the solution of philosophical problems: they are solved not by the amassing of new empirical knowledge,[3] 'but by the rearrangement of what we already know (*P.I.* I, 109)'. Given this elucidation, it is curious that Kenny should suggest in 'In Defence of God' that philosophers influenced by Wittgenstein in the philosophy of religion are imposing *alien* features on his work. If we want a contrast to Wittgenstein's conception of philosophy in the philosophy of religion, we need not look further than Kenny's own work: 'Some theologians regard religion as a way of life which can only be understood by participation and therefore cannot be justified to an outsider on neutral rational grounds. Such people must consider any attempt at a philosophical proof of God's existence to be wrong-headed, and must find it inconceivable that such matters as whether everything in motion has a mover could have relevance to religion . . . . To me it seems that if belief in the existence of God cannot be rationally justified, there can be no good grounds for adopting any of the traditional monotheistic religions.'[4] Clearly, on Kenny's own admission, Wittgenstein must be included among those who think that the desire for proofs of the existence of God is wrong-headed. Kenny also attributes to those influenced by Wittgenstein the view that only religious believers can understand religious belief. As we shall see, they do not hold such a view, but Kenny thinks, wrongly, that the only alternative to this view is the belief in the possibility of providing a neutral rational justification of religion. *Neither* thesis need be held. My aim, at the moment, however, is not to argue this point, but to clear the air regarding philosophical facts concerning Wittgenstein's influence on the philosophy of religion.

It has been argued, however, that whatever of Wittgenstein himself, those influenced by him in the philosophy of religion have gone much further than any of the emphases in Wittgenstein's work mentioned so far would warrant. They have, it is said, developed theses of their own. Any claim that these theses owe anything to Wittgenstein is an aberration on the part of those influenced by him.

Those influenced by Wittgenstein who have attempted to throw light on the nature of religious beliefs have been accused of wanting to shield religious belief against criticism. This alleged anti-intellectualism and conservatism has been given the name 'fideism', a term which, unfortunately, seems here to stay.[5] If the accounts of these critics were taken as a reliable guide to the nature of Wittgenstein's influence on the philosophy of religion, one would be led to conclude that philosophers so influenced embraced at least five theses concerning the nature of religious belief. Complaints about these theses have now been heard for almost twenty years.[6] Yet, staggering though it may seem, few have bothered to ask whether philosophers influenced by Wittgenstein have, in fact, ever propounded the five theses so confidently attributed to them. As a matter of fact, none of these theses, let alone all of them, have been held by the philosophers criticised most often in these terms. A philosophical prejudice, aided by a certain jargon, has simply generated a life of its own. It becomes necessary, therefore, to produce evidence of the misplaced character of these persistent criticisms. Since all these criticisms have been made most frequently of my work,[7] the textual evidence produced will be from that source.[8] I shall consider the five theses involved.

The first thesis attributed to philosophers influenced by Wittgenstein in the philosophy of religion is as follows: *Religious beliefs are logically cut off from all other aspects of human life*.

This is by far the most damaging claim made against philosophers of religion influenced by Wittgenstein. John Hick claims, 'The unacceptable feature of the position is that by treating religious language as autonomous – as a language-game with its own rules or a speech activity having meaning only within its own borders – it deprives religious statements of 'ontological' or 'metaphysical' significance . . . . The logical implications of religious statements do not extend across the borders of the *Sprachspiel* into assertions concerning the character of the universe beyond that fragment of it which is the religious speech of human beings. Religious language has become a kind of 'protected discourse', and forfeits its immemorial claim to bear witness to the most momentous of all truths.'[9]

The route by which this alleged thesis is supposed to be arrived at, has been discussed most fully by Walford Gealy.[10] Gealy thinks that I have misconstrued the implications of one of the central developments in Wittgenstein's later philosophy. He expounds the development he has in mind as follows: 'Throughout the *Tractatus* Wittgenstein speaks of the general form of the proposition – the form which makes it possible for language to "picture" reality. But in the *Investigations* the unity which language has is said to be informal and open-ended, and this unity is compared with that unity and relation which are all contained in the general term "games". And he emphasises that there is no one definite element which is common to all these activities.'[11] What Wittgenstein says here about language has two aspects, one of which, according to Gealy, I virtually ignore. The two aspects he has in mind are found in the following well-known passages in the *Investigations*. Here is the first:

> Consider for example the proceedings that we call 'games'. I mean board-games, card-games, ball-games, Olympic games, and so on. What is common to them all? – Don't say: 'There *must* be something common, or they would not be called "games"' – but *look and see* whether there is anything common to all. – For if you look at them you will not see something that is common to *all*, but similarities, relationships, and a whole series of them at that. To repeat: don't think, but look! – Look for example at board-games with their multifarious relationships. Now pass to card-games; here you find many correspondences with the first group, but many common features drop out, and others appear. When we pass next to ball-games, much that is common is retained, but much is lost. – Are they all 'amusing'? Compare chess with noughts and crosses. Or is there always winning and losing, or competition between players? Think of patience. In ball-games there is winning and losing; but when a child throws his ball at the wall and catches it again, this feature has disappeared. Look at the parts played by skill and luck; and at the difference between skill in chess and skill in tennis. Think now of games like ring-a-ring-a-roses; here is the element of amusement, but how many other characteristic features have disappeared! And we can go through the many, many other groups of games in the same way; we can see how similarities crop up and disappear.
>
> And the result of this examination is: we see a complicated network of similarities overlapping and criss-crossing: sometimes overall similarities, sometimes similarities of detail.[12]

Gealy also wants to call attention to the crucial preceding section where Wittgenstein writes:

> Here we come up against the great question that lies behind all these considerations. – For someone might object against me: 'You take the easy way out! You talk about all sorts of language-games, but have nowhere said what the essence of a language-game, and hence of language, is: what is common to all these activities, and what makes them into language or parts of language. So you let yourself off the very part of the investigation that once gave you yourself most headache, the part about the *general form of propositions* and of language.'
>
> And this is true. Instead of producing something common to all that we call language, I am saying that these phenomena have no one thing in common which makes us use the same word for all, – but that they are *related* to one another in many different ways. And it is because of this relationship, or these relationships, that we call them all 'language'.[13]

The two aspects of language which Gealy emphasises in these passages are as follows: first, the distinctiveness of language-games. There is no one common element which accounts for them being language-games. Thus we can make conceptual distinctions while comparing language-games. Second, the relationships between language-games: we could not have a language containing only one language-game. To belong to a language, a language-game must stand in some relation to some other language-game. This is necessary, for example, if we are to identify the language-game in question. Identity depends on contrasts and differences. On the other hand, it would be a confusion to ask how many language-games a language must contain, since that would be to assume that there are necessary and sufficent conditions for what is to count as language. This would contradict the view of the *Investigations* that the kind of unity language has is informal and open-ended.

Gealy's contention is that I stress the first aspect of language to which Wittgenstein calls our attention, but ignore the second aspect. In stressing the conceptual distinctiveness of religious beliefs, I forget, so Gealy claims, that this distinctiveness depends on the relation between religious beliefs and that which surrounds them in human life. On this view, I make religious belief an esoteric game. Different ways of speaking, different modes of language, are made absolutely autonomous. It is obvious that in these remarks Gealy is echoing the voices of many critics.

It may be thought that I myself recognise the justice of such charges. After all, in 1970, in my paper, 'Religious Beliefs and Language-Games' I made the following admission: 'I write this . . . as one who has talked of religious beliefs as distinctive language-games, but also as one who has come to feel misgivings in some respects about doing so.'[14] Later, however, I rejected this admission as premature. How, then, did I come to make it? I gave the following reason: 'I suspect that we have heard so-called fideistic . . . views attributed to us so often that we have almost come to believe in their accuracy ourselves without checking it!'[15] This is testimony enough to the hold which philosophical fashion can exert on philosophical enquiry. As a result of my suspicions, however, I underwent 'the self-inflicted penance of re-reading what I had said on these topics. I found no evidence of my having said that faith could not be challenged or overthrown by non-religious factors.'[16] Yet I cannot expect the critic to take my word for this, so what follows is a reminder of some of the ways in which I actually *oppose* the five theses which those influenced by Wittgenstein in the philosophy of religion are supposed to hold.

As early as my first book, *The Concept of Prayer*, I was anxious to stress that 'Religious concepts . . . are not *technical* concepts; they are not cut off from the common experiences of human life: joy and sorrow, hope and despair. Because this is so, an attempt can be made to clarify their meaning. The idea of prayer as talking to God presents us with this task.'[17] After all, the purpose of the whole book is to explore the connections which *do* exist between prayer and the events of human life. The fact of such connections is not contingently related to the meaning of prayer. How could God be thanked if there were nothing to thank God *for*? How could confessions be made to God if there were *nothing* to confess? How could petitions be made to God in the absence of purposes and desires? So far from denying the connections between prayer and these features of human life, I argued that if such connections are severed, the religious significance of the 'prayer' becomes problematic. I opposed writers like H. E. Fosdick, who rely on the fact that people often 'cry to God' in adversity, to prove that there is 'a spark of divinity' in all men. Whether the spark is indeed a spark of divinity depends on the part the cry plays in the life of the person concerned. Fosdick claimed that 'sometimes a crisis of danger lets loose this impulse, "I hadn't prayed in ten years", the writer heard a rail-road man exclaim when his train had just escaped a wreck; "but I prayed then".'[18] What do these prayers amount to? I replied: 'One would have to know more about each case before one could answer that question, but it is sufficient for my argument to show that unless prayers play a certain role in a person's life after the crisis is over, they are not characteristic of the *religious* role of prayer in the life of the believer. These prayers are far nearer superstition: kissing a rabbit's foot or touching wood.'[19] Compare the following examples. Bonhoeffer tells of an incident during a heavy bombing raid on a concentration camp where he was a prisoner: 'As we were all lying on the floor yesterday, someone muttered "O God, O God" – he is normally a frivolous sort of chap – but I couldn't bring myself to offer him any Christian encouragement or comfort. All I did was to glance at my watch and say: "It won't last any more than ten minutes now".'[20] Bonhoeffer did not think the man's cry was a religious cry, or that he would have understood a religious response to it. Certainly he did not think that the cry was proof that the man had 'a spark of divinity' in him. The man was obviously breaking down, and Bonhoeffer comforted him as decently as he could by telling him that the raid would soon be over. Instead of crying, 'O God, O God' the prisoner could have said 'Mamma mia' as Hemingway's dying soldier did: 'One leg was gone and the other was held by tendons and part of the trouser and the stump twitched and jerked as though it were not connected. He bit his arm and moaned, "Oh, mamma mia, mamma mia," then, "Dio ti salvi, Maria. Dio ti salvi, Maria. Oh Jesus shoot me Christ shoot me, Mamma mia, mamma mia, oh purest lovely Mary shoot me. Stop it. Stop it. Stop it. Oh Jesus lovely Mary stop it. Oh Oh Oh," then choking, "Mamma mamma mia".'[21] The cry which may take the form of a cry for God is in fact a cry for human help, or even a sheer exclamation. Whether this is so is seen, if it can be seen, from the context of the cry.

The appeal to contextual connections in determining whether responses are religious responses is no isolated emphasis confined to *The Concept of Prayer*. The same insistence is found over and over again throughout my work. I reiterate how anxious I am to show 'that religion is not some kind of technical discourse or esoteric pursuit cut off from the ordinary problems, and perplexities, hopes and joys, which most of us experience at some time or other. If it were, it would not have the importance it does have for so many people.' Taking eternal love, or the love of God, as my example, I was anxious to show in detail 'what significance it has in human experience, the kind of circumstances which occasion it, and the kind of human predicament it answers.'[22] In fact, I accused some of my critics of *their* readiness to divorce religious beliefs from their natural setting. It seemed to me then, as it does now, 'that the religious concepts discussed by Professors Hick, Hepburn and Ramsey' had 'been abstracted from the human phenomena that lie behind them, and so' had 'lost or changed their meaning'.[23]

The second thesis attributed to philosophers influenced by Wittgenstein in the philosophy of religion is as follows: *Religious beliefs can only be understood by religious believers*. Consider the following conversation between Ninian Smart and Bryan Magee:

> *Smart*: . . . That is the use of certain ideas and hints in Wittgenstein to evolve a philosophy of religion which implies that you have to believe in order to understand, so that religion is either true or meaningless. I am thinking in particular of the work of D. Z. Phillips in his *The Concept of Prayer* and some of his other writings . . . . But I am personally not altogether favourable to this approach, because it would put me out of a job, or at least out of half a job, since it would make the study of religions other than one's own, presumably – (pause)
> *Magee*: – a waste of time?
> *Smart*: A waste of time.[24]

It is clear, however, that I argue against the thesis that religious belief can only be understood by religious believers. For example, 'I am not arguing for a sharp separation between religious discourse and moral discourse. I cannot accept the account offered by some theologians which makes religion appear to be a technical language, cut off, alien and foreign to the language spoken by everyone else in the community. The picture is false and misleading. It cannot account even for religious phenomena, such as the traffic between unbelief and belief . . . . Religious doctrines, worship, ritual, etc. would not have the importance they do were they not connected with practices other than those which are specifically religious. When a man prays to God for forgiveness, for example, his prayer would be worthless did it not arise from problems in his relationships with other people. These problems can be appreciated by the religious and the non-religious alike. Because of such connections between religious and non-religious activity, *it is possible to convey the meaning of religious language to someone unfamiliar with it*, even if all one achieves is to stop him talking nonsense.'[25] But more than this may be attained. I have tried to show in my work 'that there is a vast variety of different states and attitudes within the category of religious believers, since not all believers are worshippers. A person holding any of these may see the kind of thing atheism is and still reject it. Similarly, a man may see the kind of thing religious belief is and still call himself an atheist because he does not live by such beliefs . . . . The philosopher who wants to show what kind of belief religious belief is, or what kind of attitude atheism is, may have any of these attitudes or beliefs and still fulfil his task. Indeed, he may not want to describe himself in any of these ways',[26] to call himself an atheist or a believer. True, religious believers call obedience to God a form of understanding. It would follow that anyone who did not practise such obedience in his life, lacked *that* understanding. But a philosopher can understand what I have just said about religious understanding and give an account of how obedience to God differs from other kinds of obedience, without being a believer himself, that is, in this context, without being obedient to God.

The thesis that only religious believers understand religious belief is closely connected in the minds of critics with the third and fourth theses of the five attributed to philosophers influenced by Wittgenstein in the philosophy of religion, namely, third: *Whatever is called religious language determines what is and what is not meaningful in religion*.

Kai Nielsen says, 'To be such a conceptual relativist is to argue that what is to count as knowledge, evidence, truth, a fact, an observation, making sense and the like is uniquely determined by the linguistic framework used. But since our very conception of intelligibility, validity, knowledge and the like are a function of the linguistic system we use, it is impossible for us to attain a central Archimedian point in virtue of which we could evaluate the comparative adequacy of our own and other linguistic frameworks'.[27]

And fourth: *Religious beliefs cannot be criticised*.

F. C. Coplestone says, 'The idea of autonomous language-games, each of which can be understood only from within, by those who actually play the game in question, and which is therefore immune to all external criticism, seems to me open to objection.'[28]

It is not difficult to show that these two theses, like the two already considered, are theses I have argued *against*. It would be hard to deny that 'Religious believers make mistakes like anyone else. What they say, *if* it comes under the appropriate criteria of meaningfulness, must answer to these criteria. Hick is right . . . in saying that certain conceptions of God are confused, e.g. "Yuri Gagarin's concept of God as an object that he would have observed, had it existed, during his first space flight". It can be shown to be confused in two ways: first, by reference to what one can reasonably expect to observe in space, and secondly, by what is meant by the reality of God.'[29] Nonsense remains nonsense even if we associate God's name with it. So far from wanting to deny the possibility of subjecting anything called religious to criticism, I opposed philosophical moves which ran the danger of justifying nonsense. T. H. McPherson claimed, 'Religion belongs to the sphere of the unsayable, so it is not to be wondered at that in theology there is much nonsense (i.e. many absurdities); this is the natural result of trying to put into words – and to discuss – various kinds of inexpressible "experiences", and of trying to say things about God'.[30] In response to such a view it has always seemed to me that J. A. Passmore's observation is devastatingly right: 'One difficulty with this line of reasoning, considered as a defence of religion, is that it "saves" religion only at the cost of leaving the door open to any sort of transcendental metaphysics – and indeed to superstition and nonsense of the most arrant sort.'[31] If criticism of this kind is to be avoided 'religion must take the world seriously. I have argued that religious reactions to various situations cannot be assessed according to some external criterion of adequacy. On the other hand, the connections between religious beliefs and such situations must not be fantastic . . . whether the connections are fantastic is decided by criteria which are not in dispute. For example, some religious believers may try to explain away the reality of suffering, or try to say that all suffering has some point. When they speak like this, one may accuse them of not taking suffering seriously.[32] Or if religious believers talk of death as if it were a sleep of long duration, one may accuse them of not taking death seriously.[33] In these examples, what is said about suffering and death can be judged in terms of what we already know and believe about these matters. The religious responses are fantastic because they ignore or distort what we already know. What is said falls under standards of judgement with which we are already acquainted. When what is said by religious believers does violate the facts or distort our apprehension of situations, no appeal to the fact that what is said is said in the name of religion can justify or excuse the violation or distortion.'[34]

Rationalistic philosophers of religion want to go much further than these admissions would allow. They are not content with the recognition that connections between religious beliefs and other aspects of human life may reveal confusions in religion. They want to say further, that the religious beliefs which are not confused, can be justified, inferred, or given a foundation by reference to these other aspects of human life. Indeed, it is claimed that these possibilities constitute the rationality of the beliefs. This suggestion I have resisted. Consider the following example: 'People react to the birth of children in various ways. Some say that the birth of a child is always a cause for rejoicing. Others may say that whether one rejoices at the birth of a child should be determined by the physical and mental health of the child, or by whether the family into which it is born can look after it properly. Others may say that one should always give thanks to God when a child is born. Others may condemn the folly of those responsible for bringing a child into a world such as this. All these reactions are reactions to the birth of a child, and could not mean what they do apart from the fact of the birth. But it does not follow that the various reactions can be inferred from the birth, or that they are conclusions for which the birth of the baby is the ground. All one can say is that people do respond in this way. Many who respond in one way will find the other responses shallow, trivial, fantastic, meaningless, or even evil. But the force of the responses cannot be justified; it can merely be shown.'[35]

It is a conclusion such as this, however, which has led to the fifth thesis attributed to those philosophers influenced by Wittgenstein in the philosophy of religion, namely, *Religious beliefs cannot be affected by personal, social or cultural events*.

F. C. Coplestone, speaking of the argument characterised by the four theses already considered, says, 'If it is carried to a point at which any fruitful dialogue between religious belief and critical philosophy is excluded, theology retreats into a kind of ghetto, cut off from the cultural life of which philosophy is one expression'.[36] Kenny quotes these remarks with approval.[37]

If we cannot give any rational justification for religious beliefs, does it not follow that religious beliefs have been made safe, incapable of being affected by personal, social or cultural events? No such conclusion does follow, and it is certainly not one that I have ever embraced. It cannot be denied that religious pictures which are free from conceptual confusion may nevertheless be eroded by values and developments of other kinds. Such erosion does not imply that the religious beliefs were mistakes or irrationalities of any kind. Far from denying the effects of cultural change on religious pictures I have drawn attention to them. I said we have reason 'to distinguish between the case of the picture losing its hold for a given individual, with religious pictures losing their hold anyway, not through the fault of any particular individual, but because of changes in the culture.[38] Certain religious pictures decline, and yet you can't ask "But whose fault is it that they are declining?" You can't trace the decline to the biographical details of the life of any single individual . . . a picture may die in a culture because believing it is not an isolated activity. To call the belief a language-game can be misleading if it does suggest an isolated activity. Other cultural changes can affect people's worship. For example, in *Brave New World* there is a decline in the notion of moral responsibility. In such a society one can see, without too much difficulty, how the notion of God as a Judge might also be in decline.'[39]

I have simply given textual indications of the ways in which I have argued *against* the very theses attributed to myself and others who have been influenced by Wittgenstein in the philosophy of religion. The attribution of these theses has persisted despite the availability of *all* the counter-evidence. Putting aside the fact that philosophical fashion and jargon will not be deterred by mere facts, why do these theses persist?

Nothing said so far shows why Wittgenstein's own terminology should have led to the misunderstandings we have discussed. Why should Wittgenstein's talk of language-games, for example, lead to so many misgivings among philosophers? It is with the discussion of this question that the next chapter begins.

2 Knowing Where to Stop

We saw in the last chapter that in Wittgenstein's philosophy, the urge to go beyond a certain point in a search for explanations, justifications and foundations is explored in a variety of contexts. The nature of the difficulties and temptations varies and does not form a neat unity. Nevertheless, they all involve, in some way or other, a failure to stop when one should stop. We want to ask how we know that we are seeing a tree when we are directly confronting it, how we know we are in pain while we are experiencing it, how we know others are happy when we see them jump for joy, how we know that a certain number will not occur in a mathematical progression, how we know that we are justified in drawing a statistical curve, how we know that the colour we see is red, and so on, and so on.

In all these contexts, Wittgenstein describes what he calls 'a remarkable and characteristic phenomenon in philosophical investigation: the difficulty – I might say – is not that of finding the solution but rather of recognising as the solution something that looks as if it were only a preliminary to it. "We have already said everything. – Not anything that follows from this, no, *this* itself is the solution!"

'This is connected, I believe, with our wrongly expecting an explanation, whereas the solution of the difficulty is a description, if we give it the right place in our considerations. If we dwell upon it – do not try to get beyond it.

'The difficulty here is: to stop.'[1]

We observed also in the last chapter that many commentators on Wittgenstein's work have written penetratingly on these topics, but that they are strangely silent regarding Wittgenstein's remarks on ethics and religion. Of course, there is no guarantee that what a philosopher says on various topics is equally worthwhile, and these commentators may feel that there were blind-spots in Wittgenstein's work. When they themselves write on such topics they certainly do so as if Wittgenstein had never said a word on these matters. Yet I believe that there is a more adequate explanation of their silence, one that is philosophical in character. It has to do with the hold of certain philosophical tendencies on us, a hold that is stronger than we realise. Thinking we are free of them we turn to some new field in which philosophical difficulties arise, only to find that they reassert their hold on us with all their old force. Thus we may be prepared to say with Wittgenstein in *On Certainty* that to question certain propositions which are held fast by all that surrounds them is senseless. If our trust in these propositions was undermined, if we could not show in our actions that we took these things for granted, we would not say that we were mistaken, since we wouldn't know any more what it would mean to speak of knowing, not knowing, being right or being mistaken, about such things. At certain points we say, 'But this is what I mean by saying it's a tree, a person, or a certain colour.' Or in physics we say, 'This is what I mean when I say that the conclusion is justified.' Wittgenstein asks, 'Is it wrong for me to be guided in my actions by the propositions of physics? Am I to say that I have no good ground for doing so? Isn't precisely this what we call a "good ground"?'[2] Our request for justifications in our talk about physical objects, persons, colours, and physics, comes to an end. Our assurance is shown in the way we do go on, in the way we act with respect to these things. But just as we are about to accept these conclusions, Wittgenstein juxtaposes the following example which illustrates how deep are the tendencies to resist them:

> Supposing we met people who did not regard that as a telling reason. Now, how do we imagine this? Instead of the physicist, they consult an oracle. (And for that we consider them primitive.) Is it wrong for them to consult an oracle

> and be guided by it? – If we call this 'wrong' aren't we using our language-game as a base from which to *combat* theirs?[3]

We are reluctant to say that justification must come to an end where consulting an oracle is concerned. A similar reluctance, as we have seen in the last chapter, emerges where religious beliefs are concerned. This resistance, Wittgenstein claims, is due to a misunderstanding of the nature of language-games. There is a continuity between the questions raised in *On Certainty* and Wittgenstein's 'great question',[4] which we have already discussed, namely, the question of whether one ought, having noted the multiplicity of language-games, to go on to search for something in common to them, some essence, which would make them all language. It is our desire to look beyond the language-games involved in religious beliefs and rituals which makes it difficult for us to see how Wittgenstein's full stop has any application here. We may be unable to see its application here even when we see its application elsewhere clearly.

In the last chapter we saw how philosophers have claimed that to say that Wittgenstein's full stop has any application where religious belief is concerned is to put a full stop to many commendable activities: understanding, dialogue, criticism. In this chapter I want to show how these misgivings are unjustified, do not follow from a proper reading of Wittgenstein's remarks, and take us away from the central questions which Wittgenstein was raising. First, however, let us fulfill the promise of the last chapter and see how Wittgenstein's own remarks give rise to the misgivings we outlined there.

I LANGUAGE–GAMES AND WITTGENSTEIN'S FULL STOP

Given Wittgenstein's use of the term, it makes no sense to speak of a confused language-game. H. O. Mounce reminds us that one of Wittgenstein's reasons for introducing the term 'was to free us from the idea that logic constitutes what he called "the *a priori* order of the world", the idea that logic is, as it were, "prior to all experience". He wishes us to see rather, that logic – the difference between sense and nonsense – is learnt, when, through taking part in a social life, we come to speak a language. Logic is to be found not "outside" language but only within the various language games themselves. This implies . . . that the sense of any language game cannot itself be questioned; for one could do so only on the assumption which Wittgenstein rejects, that logic does lie "outside" it.'[5] In a footnote to 'the sense of any language game cannot itself be questioned', Mounce adds, 'The "cannot", of course, is logical. I do not mean that if one tried one would fail, but that it would be senseless to try.'[6] Now if one argues that there are distinctive language-games involved in rituals and religious beliefs it makes no sense to question their sense. This claim seems to run counter to what actually happens. Surely people do respond to religious beliefs by saying, 'That belief makes no sense' or 'I no longer see anything in that belief'. So it seems that if one does say that there are distinctive language-games associated with rituals and religion, one at the same time protects those rituals and that religion from criticism. But religious beliefs and practices *are* criticised. To interpret Wittgenstein's remarks on language-games in the way suggested is to indulge, it seems, in conservatism and protectionism. Anthony Kenny, fearing such consequences, says, 'The concept of language-games is an obscure and ambiguous one in Wittgenstein's own writings: in the hands of some of his religious admirers it has become a stone-wall defence against any demand for a justification of belief in God'.[7]

At this point, it is very tempting to take a short-cut out of our difficulties. One could do so by suggesting that we must make a distinction between the notion of a language-game on the one hand, and the notion of a mode of discourse or a practice on the other. By means of such a contrast we can construct a normative view of language-games. Modes of discourse or practices could then be criticised if in fact they distort language-games in some way or other. On this view it seems that language-games are, in some sense, 'prior' to modes of discourse and practices. Already we see that we are dangerously close, despite using Wittgenstein's terminology, to the very conception of logic Wittgenstein wanted to reject, namely, the idea of logic as somehow 'prior' to all experience. The attraction of the view is that it allows us to criticise practices and modes of discourse. It would no longer be sufficient to appeal to the fact that certain ways of talking are moral or religious modes of discourse to avoid the charge of senselessness.

This attempted distinction between language-games on the one hand, and modes of discourse or practices on the other, is found in the following view-point embraced by Richard Bell: 'Language has a variety of uses, and people who speak a language frequently use that language for religious purposes.'[8] But what does it mean to speak of language being *used for religious purposes*? Is it like saying that an argument is used for political or prudential purposes, where the status of the argument is quite distinct from the purposes for which it is employed? Consider another contrast. Could we say that the only difference between moral and prudential commendation is the different purposes for which the concept of commendation is employed? Wittgenstein would not have agreed with this way of putting the matter. Wittgenstein, in his 'Lecture on Ethics', wants to distinguish between what he calls 'absolute' and 'relative' uses of 'ought'. So if we compare 'You ought to keep your matches dry' and 'You ought to treat her decently', are we to say that we have here two instances of doing the same thing – of commending? The difficulty for such a view is that the moral context makes a difference to what the commending comes to. Bell wants to say of religion, what he would probably say of ethics also, namely, that 'uses of language . . . do not convert the status of "utterances", "assertions" or "expressions" to a different level of linguistic understanding . . . . Thus when "religious" is used with "language" it should draw our attention to the fact that certain concepts are being used for religious purposes, and not that some kind of semantic or substantive shift has been made to a new type of discourse.'[9] But this cannot be said of the moral use of 'ought'. We cannot say that *the* concept is used for moral purposes, since it is only in the context of these so-called purposes that the concept has its distinctive grammatical status. We cannot distinguish between the language-game and the moral issues about which commendations are made, since it is precisely the character of the issues which affect the character of the commendation. But do religious beliefs have a distinctive grammatical status? Bell's paper contains an admission of such grammatical distinctions, but he does not seem to realise the significance of the admission for his more general comments: ' "Asking, thanking, cursing, greeting, praying": In theological and religious behaviour these language-games usually have liturgical functions which only partially parallel their ordinary use.'[10] But if, for example, 'talking to God' functions in ways which are importantly different from, let us say, talking to another person, we cannot say that we have *the* concept of talking which is used for religious, as well as other purposes. So this short-way with our difficulties does not succeed.

Another, more subtle, but equally unsatisfactory attempt at a short-way with our difficulties can be found in a further attempt to distinguish between language-games and practices. This view does not involve a normative view of language-games. Language-games are not thought of as in any sense 'prior' to practices. The distinctive suggestion advanced is that Wittgenstein usually meant by language-games, not a practice, but a set of concepts which run through almost any conceivable practice. It is not denied that distinctive language-games may be involved in modes of discourse or practices. What *is* denied is that we can identify *every* practice with a language-game. Such an identification would preclude the possibility of speaking of confused practices. However pervasive a practice, it may still be confused. H. O. Mounce puts forward the proposed distinction between language-games and practices as follows:

> When we speak of our certainty that another person is in pain, for example, we play a different game from when we speak of our certainty that there is a table in the next room. Now . . . it would be difficult to suppose that what Wittgenstein here means by a language game is anything like a practice such as conducting scientific experiments or worshipping in church. For example, one may speak of people coming together to conduct a scientific experiment but hardly of their coming together to exercise the concept of pain; one may speak of a person giving up religious worship but not of his giving up the use of the notion of an object. What we here mean by a language game is not a practice or set of practices but a set of concepts which may enter into almost any practice we can imagine.[11]

As we shall see, there are serious difficulties in Mounce's attempt to draw a distinction between language-games and practices in Wittgenstein's work. Yet, these apart, how true in general of the examples Wittgenstein provides is the way in which Mounce speaks of language-games? Mounce suggests that his distinction between language-games and practices reflects in general the character of the examples:

> For example, one instance of a language game is giving an order. Now if a person gives an order one may say that he is performing an action but hardly that he is engaged in an activity or practice. One may say, it is true, that an order can be given in the *course* of an activity. The point is, however, that in saying this, one does not have any particular activity in mind. Almost any activity can be the occasion for giving an order. Similar remarks apply to most of Wittgenstein's other examples.[12]

The first thing to be said is that this is an overstatement and over-simplification of Wittgenstein's notion of language-games. That it is an overstatement can be seen from the examples of language-games Wittgenstein provides.[13] While one has examples such as 'Giving orders and obeying them', 'Asking', 'Thanking', etc., one also has examples such as 'Presenting the results of an experiment in tables and diagrams' and 'Solving a problem in practical arithmetic'. Wittgenstein says that the instances are countless and extremely varied. Nor will it do to say that what giving an order amounts to always comes to the same thing. 'What the general commands', 'What the gods command', and 'What the state commands' are importantly different. I mean that the grammar of 'command' is importantly different in each case. This can be illustrated by Wittgenstein's own examples of language-games. He gives the following list: 'Asking, thanking, cursing, greeting, praying'.[14] Clearly, praying, worshipping, is an example of an activity which is also called a language-game. It makes sense to speak of people coming together for this purpose, and of their giving up praying. But, more importantly, we cannot say without qualification of asking, thanking and cursing that whereas they can occur in the course of a wider activity, one need not have any particular activity in mind. Failure to keep in mind the activity in question may lead to the ignoring of important conceptual differences. For example, it is obvious that one asks and thanks for things in prayer. It is also the case that people have cursed God. If the activity of praying made no conceptual difference to what asking and thanking amount to, its inclusion in the list of language-games would be superfluous. It cannot be said that the difference between asking God for something and asking another human being for something resides in the resources of the person to whom the request is made, since this would not introduce any *conceptual* change into the nature of the asking. The presence of prayer in the list of language-games means that Wittgenstein thought that some conceptual distinction is involved. I have explored this conceptual difference elsewhere and suggested that to ask and thank in prayer is to come to a certain kind of understanding of those features of our lives which prompt our gratitude and ingratitude and occasion our desires.[15] Similarly, conceptual differences would emerge from a comparison of cursing God with cursing another human being. Just as we can say, 'My friend forgives me, but I cannot forgive myself', but not, 'God forgives me, but I cannot forgive myself', so in one context, at least, one can curse another person and still find life meaningful, whereas to curse God is to curse the day that one was born.

For the above reasons, Mounce's distinction between language-games and practices will not do. Furthermore, Mounce's distinction obscures the importance of the notion of practice in Wittgenstein. We do not have language-games which run through practices or occur in the course of them. 'Practice', 'activity', 'what we do', in Wittgenstein is not something *apart* from language-games, since the latter are themselves forms of activity, practice. For example, we cannot separate the conceptual distinctions involved in the language-games we play with colours or pains from the ways in which we react and respond, since the concepts are themselves rooted in these common reactions and responses, by these practices. Without the common practices, there would be no concepts concerning colours or pains. To see what is meant by the reality of God, we must take note of the concept formation by which the notion of the divine is rooted in the reactions of praise and worship. That is why, in *The Concept of Prayer*, I argued against the philosophical tradition which assumes that one ought to determine first whether God exists before considering the grammar of worship. From *The Concept of Prayer* to *Religion Without Explanation* I have denied that philosophy can determine *whether* there is a God. On the other hand, I have also emphasised the futility of thinking that we can see what is *meant* by the reality of God in isolation from the context of worship and praise.

If we cannot seek short-ways with our difficulties by distinguishing between language-games on the one hand and modes of discourse or practices on the other hand, as Bell, Mounce, and others have suggested, is it not the case that all our problems remain? If we say that religious beliefs and rituals involve distinctive language-games which are rooted in and expressed in practices, does it not follow that no room has been allowed for criticism of these practices?

II RITUALS, BELIEFS AND APPLICATIONS IN HUMAN LIFE

Let us now try to approach our difficulty from another direction. Wittgenstein insisted that each language-game is complete. A language-game is not a partial or confused attempt to indicate something else to which it approximates. But this very claim of completeness with respect to language-games involved with rituals and religion has again led people to feel that this puts a full stop to any interaction between religious practices and other features of human life. These practices begin to look more like esoteric games, just as, if one thinks of building activity as similarly cut off from all that surrounds it, it begins to look more like a game with building blocks.[16]

Here the analogy between language and games begins to limp, since although we do not say that all games make up one big game, we do say that people engaged in various language-games are engaged in the same language. It is clear that many of the language-games we do play would not have the sense that they do were there not other language-games independent of them. This is certainly true of rituals and religious practices. One could not have songs and dances concerning the harvest unless, independent of such songs and dances, one had activities concerning the harvest, sowing and reaping, conceptions of good and bad harvests, and so on. We have already noted, in the previous chapter, how prayers would have no substance were there nothing to *occasion* prayer or for prayer to be *about*.

If, however, we admit all this, must we not also admit that there is two-way traffic involved? Just as various events and activities in human life can be celebrated in ritual or brought before God in prayer, may not the aspects of rituals and prayers themselves be changed by these various events and activities? And if this is admitted, may not their aspect change for the worse sometimes; may not confusions and distortions set in? *May they not cease to be distinctive language-games*? These questions must be answered in the affirmative, but there is no reason to think that Wittgenstein cannot allow such an answer. On the contrary, one cannot ascribe to Wittgenstein the view that anything that is called religious or ritualistic is free from confusion.[17] That much is clear from the following:

> We should distinguish between magical operations and those operations which rest on a false, over-simplified notion of things and processes. For instance, if someone says that the illness is moving from one part of the body into another, or if he takes measures to draw off the illness as though it were a liquid or a temperature. He is then using a false picture, a picture that doesn't fit.[18]

Wittgenstein, apparently, had in mind here quack doctors and certain kinds of faith-healing. But he *also* thought that confusion could be found in practices which did not purport to be substitutes for science. Wittgenstein began an earlier version of his remarks on Frazer by saying, 'I think now that the right thing would be to start my book with remarks on metaphysics as a kind of magic.'[19] To illustrate what Wittgenstein had in mind, contrast acupuncture with sticking pins in an effigy. Acupuncture may have various consequences, some good, some bad. But whatever one's view of its status, it clearly aims at achieving ends similar to those of other medical methods. But sticking pins in an effigy may not have an aim in that sense, any more than a war-dance is conducting a war. How, then, does a ritual tell us something? Here the distinction between a language-game and a form of life is important in Wittgenstein. How the language-games – certain ritualistic songs and dances, say – are taken depends on their connections with other things. They do not have meaning in themselves, any more than the act of pointing does. To think otherwise is to adopt what Wittgenstein would call a magical view of meaning. This larger context of human life, in which we see how a language game is taken, Wittgenstein calls a form of life. The notion of a form of life is essential in seeing in what sense a ritual can say something.

The ritual may contain words and gestures peculiar to the ritual, but it will also contain words and gestures which have an application in the non-ritualistic contexts of life. Without this application the ritual could not have its power and force. Without it, as we have seen, it becomes an esoteric game. And yet this notion of the power of the ritual may breed confusion: the idea that the power resides in the words themselves, a common idea where magic is concerned. The confusion involved may be akin to metaphysical confusion. Consider the following example:

> I point with my hand and say 'Come here.' A asks 'Did you mean me?' I say 'No, B.' – What went on when I meant B (since my pointing left it in no doubt which I meant)? – I said those words, made that gesture. Must still more have taken place, in order for the language-game to take place? But didn't I already know, while I was pointing, whom I meant? Know? Of course – going by the usual criteria of knowledge.[20]

The confusion here is the desire to follow 'He meant B' with the question, 'How does he mean B?' expecting an answer in terms of a process or power which somehow accompanies the words, or in terms of some inherent power in the act of pointing. Understanding lies in seeing that meaning depends on the shared application that the words and the gestures have in this context. A similar confusion may arise in rituals in thinking that the power lies in the words or in the gestures: the curse is spoken, the wizard points, the man falls.

To see how the ritual speaks one must take account of its application in human life. Compare the following:

> For how can it be explained what 'expressive playing' is? Certainly not by anything that accompanies the playing – What is needed for the explanation? One might say: a culture. – If someone is brought up in a particular culture – and then reacts to music in such-and-such a way, you can teach him the use of the phrase, 'expressive playing'.[21]

What we need to bring in to show how a ritual says something is its role in a culture. That role in magic and religion has much to do with the formal character of the ritual. Certain features of everyday life are formalised, set apart, celebrated at set times, solstices, equinoxes, phases of the moon, birth, death, harvest; the exact words are to be repeated in the exact order, surrounded by sanctions and responses of distinctive kinds. It is this application in human life which is important, but which, as in the case of the gesture, 'Come here' or expressive playing, may be distorted if it is thought that the power is an inherent property of the words, something accompanying them as it were. The temptation to think this is aided and strengthened if the ritual does contain gestures and words which, in non-ritualistic circumstances, *would* be instances of ways of attaining certain ends. Wittgenstein warns us of this as follows: 'Do not forget that a poem, even though it is composed in the language of information is not used in the language-game of giving information.'[22] What underlies the temptation to think otherwise in these examples may be akin to what underlies the temptation towards the metaphysical conclusion about the connection between words and meanings. This is *one* way in which a connection might be established between magic and metaphysics.[23]

Consider another example. In Leviticus we are told that on the Day of Atonement, a goat said to be laden with the sins of the people is driven into the wilderness, the abode of Azazel, leader of the evil angels. As the scapegoat is driven into the wilderness, so the sins of the people depart with it to the spirits of darkness to whom they belong. Rhees points out that some months before he began the first comments on Frazer, Wittgenstein wrote, 'The scapegoat on which sins are laid and which goes out into the wilderness with them, is a false picture, like all the false pictures of philosophy. Philosophy might be said to purify thought from a misleading mythology' (*MS* 109, 210f.). I shall quote at length Rhees' comment on this ritual:

'In the rite of the scapegoat (Leviticus 16:20–2) several analogies come together. It would be natural in a tribal society to speak of "bearing the sins of others": of a family sharing the sin committed by any member of it, or of children bearing the sins of their forefathers. The sins of the people come between them and God. But purification was possible through sacrifice, and then the people could turn to God again for help. Here there are metaphors enough, but they need not mislead anyone. Suppose then: "If the people assembled here do bear the sins of their fathers, and of their brothers now living, then why should not the priest bring in some animal to be made one of them in this sense only – that it bears their sins – and then, after laying his hands on it, send it with their sins away from them into the wilderness?" When Wittgenstein calls this rite a misleading picture, he may mean something like this: consider

1 "Children carry the sins of their fathers."
2 "A goat, when consecrated, carries the sins of the people."

In the first sentence "carry" is used in the sense of the whole sentence. In the second sentence "carry" seems to mean what it does in "The goat carries on his back the basket in which we put our firewood"; and yet it *cannot* mean that.

Of course a living animal may be taken as a symbol together with the other symbols, the symbolic performance, in the ritual. But in this case Wittgenstein thought the symbol, in the role that was given to it, was badly misleading.

(If we called it an *incongruous* simile, we should be speaking in a different tongue and a different culture; we should be saying how the account of this strikes us now. Perhaps we should not find it incongruous – we should not find the picture jars in symbolizing what is intended for it – if you said that a *man* might take on himself the sins the people had to bear, and offer himself in atonement for them. But a goat? What would it mean to say that a goat has to bear its *own* sins, let alone that it has to bear the sins of *people*? Bunyan's image of Christian bearing his sins like a heavy pack on his shoulders does not jar in this way. I am bewildered by the separate roles of the two goats in the rituals described in Leviticus. The goat that takes on itself the sins of the people is not killed and sacrificed in an offering to God. The people may have looked on the goat that was slaughtered as something they offered in place of their first born – as Abraham saw the ram that God told him to offer in place of his son. But it is hard to see the substitution in the scapegoat that delivers them of their sins. I do not know how they thought of this. Nor does anyone now. This does not affect the point Wittgenstein is making.)'[24]

Consider the following comment on the same ritual which, to some extent, but not entirely, recognises the difficulty:

> On the ritual of the scapegoat, Matthew Henry observes that it 'had been a jest, nay an affront to God, if he himself had not ordained it' . . . But in these days can we any longer say that God ordained it? Ritual may be a substitute for true religion or it may be its natural and spontaneous expression . . . . Men may take a magical view of the sacraments, as of such rites as the scapegoat . . . It is obvious that sins could not really be transferred to a goat. But can sins be transferred at all? . . . Christ, as identified with man in his shame and sin, rejected by men and driven away bearing their sins and done to death for their forgiveness, is symbolically depicted, crudely and inadequately yet really, in the scapegoat.[25]

Notice that here one has the possibility of criticism within a tradition. The ritual concerning the scapegoat is called crude and inadequate. Wittgenstein might say that the crudity and inadequacy are partly connected, at least, with the confusion in the role attributed to an animal in the ritual. By thinking that the scapegoat *can* take away sins, the legitimate longing of a people to be freed from their sins is obscured and distorted. What 'being freed from sin' amounts to, how it is taken and understood, changes accordingly; it may take on a magical significance. The prophets, of course, criticised such magical conceptions of rituals. Mechanistic views of participation in the Eucharist have been subjected to similar criticisms. Compare how a belief that one's sins are washed away by bathing in a holy river may develop in diverse directions, some religious, others superstitious. A mechanistic view of what it is to lose one's sins in such a context may go hand in hand with conferring quasi-causal properties on the river. The power of baptism in the river, let us say, for the remission of sins, may be partly confused in much the same way as the idea that the efficacy of a phrase resides in its inherent power: a baptism of meaning. In saying that the symbolism of the scapegoat jars, Wittgenstein can be taken as showing how reflection and criticism within religion may have affinities with the discussion of philosophical confusions.[26]

In the light of our considerations in this section of the essay, we can see that nothing Wittgenstein says about language-games and their implications for practices and modes of discourse implies that confusions of various kinds cannot enter into religious beliefs and rituals. We can see how unfounded are Coplestone's fears, referred to in the last chapter, of a lack of fruitful dialogue between religious belief and critical philosophy being a consequence of Wittgenstein's views. Similarly, we can see how Passmore's reaction to the distinction between different modes of discourse is misplaced when he says that it 'has recently attracted a good many admirers, particularly amongst those who desire to be uncritically religious without ceasing to be critically philosophical.'[27]

As we have seen, Wittgenstein's views do not rule out the possibility of criticism of religion. To show how such criticism is possible, however, what we need is not a variety of dubious distinctions between language-games, modes of discourse and practices, but a consideration of what may happen to certain language-games in the course of their application in human life.[28]

III THE NON-DERIVABILITY OF LANGUAGE-GAMES AND THE DESIRE FOR EXPLANATION

In the previous section we have seen how certain misunderstandings can arise from Wittgenstein's claim that language-games are complete in themselves. Yet, despite these misunderstandings, which help to bring out certain limits to the analogy between language and games, they do not affect Wittgenstein's insistence on the non-derivability of language-games. Acknowledging the limitations in the analogy should not lead to the view put forward by Hepburn, Hick and Nielsen, namely, that the distinctive language-games found in religion and rituals stand themselves in need of a further justification, foundation or even verification. It is tempting to assume that since some practices may be confused, those which are free from confusion must be so by virtue of being well-founded. This temptation must be resisted. To say that the force of a religious or ritualistic response cannot be appreciated in isolation from the form of life of which that response is a part is not to say that there must be a further justification of the response. As we saw in the last chapter, the response need not be related to that which surrounds it as a hypothesis is related to the evidence for it, as a conclusion is related to its premisses, or as a belief is related to its reasons.[29] Once the response is elucidated we can say no more from within philosophy than, 'Human life is like that'. Our task is a descriptive one. In this task Wittgenstein's big question about language will keep coming up, since there will always be the temptation to think that what we have before us are incomplete forms of expression awaiting completion in a wider system.

In his 'Remarks on Frazer's *The Golden Bough*', Wittgenstein was simply examining one form which the urge to regard expressions in ritual as incomplete may take. There are important connections between Wittgenstein's remarks on Frazer and his remarks on Schlick's *Ethics*. Although in 1930 Wittgenstein still speaks of ethics as thrusting against the limits of language, he also says that he regards it 'as very important to put an end to all the chatter about ethics'. What he meant by this principally was the recurring attempt to give values a foundation, an explanation. Speaking of such explanations he says, 'Whatever one said to me I would reject it; not indeed because the explanation is false, but because it is an *explanation*.'[30] Similarly, Wittgenstein's reason for rejecting Frazer's explanations is not because they are false, but because they are explanations, and as such take us away from the philosophically arresting features of the rituals he is discussing. In the earlier set of remarks on Frazer, written about 1931, Wittgenstein speaks as though we *already* have in our possession, in the language we speak, a principle by which any practices we come across can be ordered and assessed. As Rhees points out in his Introductory Note, however, by the time Wittgenstein comes to his second set of remarks, at least five years later, he does not speak in this way. Here, to imagine a ritual is to imagine it in a form of life.

Rhees says: 'It will in fact be helpful if we *do* hold on to the kinship between ritual and language here, not because ritual is a form of language, but because in order to understand *language* it is *also* necessary to look to the lives of the people who take part in it. What we call language, or what we call "*saying something*" is not determined by some "knowledge of the language" which each of us carries "within his own mind". What *I* would call "saying something", perhaps because it is correctly formed or constructed on every count, would *not* be "saying something" unless it had what Wittgenstein called "an application in our life".'[31]

When this application is considered, it should put an end to the chatter about rituals, just as it should put an end to the chatter about ethics. When this is appreciated, philosophical clarity is achieved. Drury brings out the matter well:

> Frazer thinks he can make *clear* the origin of the rites and ceremonies he describes by regarding them as primitive and erroneous scientific beliefs. The words he uses are, 'We shall do well to look with leniency upon the errors as inevitable slips made in the search for truth'. Now Wittgenstein made it clear to me that on the contrary the people who practised these rites already possessed a considerable scientific achievement, agriculture, metalworking, building, etc., etc.; and the ceremonies existed alongside these sober techniques. They are not mistaken beliefs that produced the rites but the need to express something; the ceremonies were a form of language, a form of life. Thus today if we are introduced to someone we shake hands; if we enter a church we take off our hats and speak in a low voice; at Christmas perhaps we decorate a tree. These are expressions of friendliness, reverence, and of celebration. We do not believe that shaking hands has any mysterious efficacy, or that to keep one's hat on in church is dangerous! Now this I regard as a good illustration of how I understand clarity as something to be desired as a goal, as distinct from clarity as something to serve a further elaboration. For seeing these rites as a form of language immediately puts an end to all the elaborate theorising concerning 'primitive mentality'. The clarity prevents a condescending misunderstanding, and puts a full-stop to a lot of idle speculation.[32]

The urge for explanation is, however, deep-rooted. Having perhaps rid ourselves of the view of rituals and rites as theories or erroneous scientific beliefs, we can easily come to look for psychological explanations of the same phenomena.

In Drury's remarks, for example, we find him talking of certain forms of behaviour as *expressions* of friendliness, reverence and celebration. But he also speaks of rites as the results of *a need to express something*. This too savours of an explanation. It makes it look as if the rites are the *means* by which something is expressed, as though there were a distinction between means and ends involved. Speaking of burning an effigy, Wittgenstein says, 'Burning an effigy. Kissing the picture of a loved one. This is obviously *not* based on a belief that it will have a definite effect on the object which the picture represents.' At first, Wittgenstein says of each of these actions, 'It aims at some satisfaction and it achieves it', but then he corrects himself immediately: 'Or rather, it does not aim at anything; we act in this way and then feel satisfied.'[33] A man does not smash the portrait of his beloved *in order* to express his anger. This is the form his anger takes. Whether the rites are regarded as erroneous scientific beliefs or as psychologically instrumental, these explanations take us away from the important features of the rites which philosophy should concentrate on. G. K. Chesterton comments as follows:

> . . . even where the fables are inferior as art, they cannot be properly judged by science; still less properly judged as science. Some myths are very crude and queer like the early drawings of children; but the child is trying to draw. It is none the less an error to treat his drawing as if it were a diagram, or intended to be a diagram. The student cannot make a scientific statement about the savage, because the savage is not making a scientific statement about the world. He is saying something quite different; what might be called the gossip of the gods. We may say, if we like, that it is believed before there is time to examine it. It would be truer to say that it is accepted before there is time to believe it.[34]

Chesterton is not saying, of course, that the acceptance is premature. He is reminding us rather of the *character* of the acceptance, of what Wittgenstein would call the primitive response. He is insisting that the grammar of religious belief should be explored in the context of such responses. Chesterton is bringing out the naturalness of religious responses, a naturalness which explanations obscure from us. It is extremely important to note, however, that this naturalness is naturalness *within a culture*. Deep confusions may result from misrepresentations of what this implies. Thus, having said that 'The weeping-willow, taken by the Elizabethans as a symbol of unhappy love, does resemble in its lines the drooping and hanging hands', Edwyn Bevan goes on to say that 'if convention had once made a holly-bush instead of a weeping-willow the symbol of unhappy love, an association would in time be created in the mind between them, so that the sight of holly would immediately suggest the other'.[35] This makes it look as if the significance of the weeping-willow were a function of a rule of association consisting in no more than a constant conjunction decreed by convention. What this obscures completely is the naturalness of seeing a connection between the weeping-willow and the drooping gait. A failure to see this is not a failure of knowledge of an associative rule, but a failure of imagination. The explanation is also misleading in giving the impression that seeing the weeping-willow as we do is a matter of choice, something we could take up or drop at will. Bevan almost suggests that we could choose whether to make the imaginative projection from human sadness with respect to a holly-bush rather than a weeping-willow.

The misunderstandings in the urge for explanations of religious responses are well illustrated in Bevan's chapter on 'Height'. He tries to give various explanations of why divinity has often been expressed in terms of height. He speculates, for example, that since commanders needed to get on high land to see the sweep of the land, those in authority became associated with height; they were to be looked up to. Again, someone might say that height and the divine become associated because of a prior association of height with authority. Kings and thrones are placed on high. This simply postpones the issue. Why are they placed on *high*? Again, the explanations take us away from the naturalness of the expression, a naturalness shown in the vision of the Divine Being which the prophet Isaiah expresses as 'sitting on a throne high and lifted up'. Here we have the language of exaltation. Bevan approaches a recognition of the naturalness of this way of talking when he says that 'the idea of height, as an essential characteristic of supreme worth, was so interwoven in the very texture of all human languages that it is impossible for us even today to give in words a rendering of what was meant by the metaphor. We are inevitably forced, if we try to explain the metaphor, to bring in the very metaphor to be explained.'[36] He is not content to rest with the expression as a natural response in a culture and proceeds, in some ways absurdly, to try to explain it:

> Of those symbols which are taken from the outside material world the significance of height seems to have come to men everywhere immediately and instinctively. We may feel it today so obvious as not to call for any explanation. And yet if one fixes the attention on what height literally is, the reason for this universal instinct seems problematic. For height literally is nothing but the distance from the earth's surface in a direction at right angles outwards. The proposition: Moral and spiritual worth is greater or less in ratio to the distance outwards from the earth's surface, would certainly seem to be, if stated nakedly like that, an odd proposition. And yet that is the premiss which seems implied in this universal association of height with worth and with the Divine.[37]

Bevan does not realise the import of his own remarks when he speaks of the expressive uses of height in connection with divinity not calling for explanation. For Bevan, these uses are problematic, whereas in fact what is problematic is his own insistence that we must fix our attention on what height 'literally' is. He was ignoring what Wittgenstein calls the mythology in our language, a mythology in this case which has far less to do with spatial height than some people have supposed. Rather than speak so much of conceptions of the divine as superfluous, because of changing conceptions of the universe, (which is not to deny the influence of such changes), we should look at our primitive reactions in reaching out for something, and the fact that elation is a rising and dejection a falling, in order to see how concept formation concerning aspiration to, and exaltation of, what is on high gets off the ground. What if people discontinued believing that 'the one on high' dwelt in the mountains once they had climbed them? Does *that* show that they cannot believe that some kind of *thing* dwells in the mountains because of a failure to locate it, so necessitating the placing of the worshipped one higher, beyond the clouds? Hardly. What has happened is that looking to the mountains for the one on high loses its expressive force when one has mastered the mountains by climbing them. The mastery of the mountain makes impossible one form of expressive reaction; an impossibility which itself may lead to the further reaction: the one we look to is higher than the mountains.[38] What we are offered here is not explanation, but elucidation. But in such elucidations we do not dispense with imaginative projections. On the contrary, we elucidate some by putting others alongside them. To be aware of this mythology in our language and to see the naturalness of its connection with religious beliefs and rituals is to give up asking why these things happen, why they are believed, or whether these expressions in language correspond to reality. Such enquiries are brought to a full stop.

We are now in a position to see that what I have called Wittgenstein's full stop has nothing to do with any attempt, subtle or otherwise, to shield religion from criticism. We have seen, on the contrary, that nothing Wittgenstein says prevents the exposure of confused practices, however pervasive, or prohibits criticism of or within religious traditions.

Further, it is important to see that Wittgenstein's remarks

leave criticism of another kind precisely where it is. Having seen what religious beliefs and rituals come to, someone may still want to make moral criticisms of them. Nothing Wittgenstein says restricts such criticism. Wittgenstein's remarks are also neutral with respect to whether we should or should not want to see these practices flourish or decline and work to that end. When Wittgenstein says that he would not call the practice of consulting oracles wrong, he does not deny that people may want to combat the practice. On the contrary, he says that that is what they do when they oppose it. He asks us to think of what happens when missionaries convert natives.[39] Wittgenstein is not denying the fact of conversion from one view or belief to another. He is asking us to reflect on what that comes to. In particular he is asking us to see that it does not necessitate the postulation of a wider system in which the warring beliefs are contradictions. Think of the temptation to assume that when Callicles accused Socrates of passing off on his audience a low popular conception of what is fine, there must be a wider ethical system in which the views of Callicles and Socrates are contradictories. When Wittgenstein says that language-games are complete he is resisting the postulation of a wider system of which they are the parts.

Similarly, nothing Wittgenstein says denies the possibility of religious beliefs or rituals losing their sense for an individual or in a culture. Wittgenstein says that 'new language-games . . . come into existence, and others become obsolete and get forgotten.'[40] But what loss of sense amounts to involves many things.[41] A man may lose his faith, fail to see the sense in it, because it proves too hard for him. Other things win his allegiance. He finds, for example, that he cannot serve God and Mammon. The more Mammon interests him, the less sense he sees in serving God. Such loss of faith may become a pervasive feature of a society as a result of certain things becoming prestigious within it. Nothing Wittgenstein has said denies these possibilities. Neither would he deny that bad philosophy may bring about a loss of faith. A man may lose the sense of his faith because he comes to believe the stipulations of philosophers about the sense it must have. On the other hand, in other circumstances, shielding belief from intellectual enquiry may itself be a sign of religious, as well as intellectual, insecurity.

It may be said, however, that there is one kind of criticism of religious beliefs and practices which Wittgenstein will not allow, namely, the kind of criticism one finds in Frazer. He would also reject the kind of request for foundations and verifications found in Nielsen, Hick and others. Neither could he regard religious belief as an ideology or illusion awaiting explanation in the styles of Marx or Freud. Therefore, it may be said, he does not leave all criticism where it is. Even if this were true, it would not be because it is *criticism*, but because it is bad philosophy, bad philosophy concerning logic. But the charge is not even true, since it cannot be said that Wittgenstein rules out *any* genuine form of criticism. What he does not allow is something which purports to be criticism, but which is itself a species of philosophical confusion.[42] A philosopher can hardly be expected to leave bad philosophy where it is. What Wittgenstein does not leave where it is are certain forms of rationalism and scientism, and the criticisms, justifications and explanations of religion emanating from them.

What is to guide us in the rejection of these confused tendencies? Wittgenstein would say: what already lies before us, what we know when not philosophising. We need to reflect on these things. But are there special difficulties facing such philosophical procedures where religion is concerned? That is the issue which we have to face in the next chapter.

3 Reminders of What We Know?

We ended the last chapter by stating that in the philosophy of religion there may be special problems posed for some of the central features of Wittgenstein's philosophical techniques. Let us remind ourselves of Kenny's depiction of these features: 'In saying that in philosophy there are no deductions Wittgenstein set himself against the type of philosophy which offers proofs, e.g. of the existence of God or immortality of the soul . . . . Throughout his life he remained sceptical of and hostile to philosophy of that kind. "We must do away with all explanation" he wrote "and description alone must take its place." The point of the description is the solution of philosophical problems: they are solved not by the amassing of new empirical knowledge',[1] 'but by arranging what we have always known' (*P.I.*, 109). Yet, when we turn to the philosophy of religion, additional problems await us. These have been brought out well by O. K. Bouwsma in his comparison and contrast of the philosophical tasks facing Kierkegaard and Wittgenstein. Like Kenny, Bouwsma says, 'In the works of Wittgenstein there is ordinary language we understand. That ordinary language is related to words and expressions that give us trouble. In ordinary language we discover the corrective of that language which expresses the confusion.'[2] When we turn to Kierkegaard we may think, at first, that we have an exact parallel. After all, 'The task in both cases is conceived as that of dispelling illusions. The illusion is in both cases one of misunderstanding certain languages . . . . Both those who seek to understand ordinary language, and those who seek to understand the scriptures run into confusion due to mistaken conceptions concerning what the language must mean.'[3] Wherein, then, does the difference lie? 'In the work of Kierkegaard there corresponds to ordinary language in Wittgenstein the language of scriptures, which Kierkegaard understands. Without this latter assumption Kierkegaard cannot be effective. And this is not how it is in Wittgenstein. There ordinary language is taken to be language which we all understand. Here there is agreement. But Kierkegaard's task is in that way more formidable. He has first to teach us the language of scripture.'[4] In the light of these remarks, the observation that philosophical problems are resolved 'by arranging what we have always known' has to be reconsidered. Bouwsma is calling attention to the fact that we (all of us) do *not* already know what the scriptures mean, if only because, for many people, the scriptures mean nothing, play no part in their lives. At first it may be thought that this presents no problem for what Wittgenstein is saying. After all, if a philosopher does not have any use for religion when not philosophising, how can that religious use mislead him while philosophising? The answer is simple: people do not restrict their philosophisings to themes or concepts for which they have a use when not philosophising. Philosophers who stand in no personal relationship to religion may still philosophise about it, especially if they are looking for Kenny's neutral rational justifications of it.

Still, even here, the philosopher's failure to see any sense in religion may still be due to mistaken expectations of what language must mean if it is to mean anything at all. And would not the possibility of removing these expectations, and getting rid of the dogmatism which thinks it knows what language *must* be if it is to be meaningful, itself depend on reflecting on what we (some people) know about the character of religious beliefs and rituals? It is worth emphasising again, in passing, that coming to appreciate the grammar of these religious beliefs does not entail coming to believe in them. Even after a philosopher rids himself of mistaken expectations about what beliefs *must* be, so that he comes to appreciate something of the character of religious belief, it still does not follow, nor need it follow, that he can make sense of his own life in these terms.

Yet can the point Bouwsma was making be accommodated so easily? In the reply offered, reflection on examples, whether the confused philosopher is aware of them initially or not, is reflection on examples from religious life and literature. Can we assume *in vacuo*, however, that such reflection is always possible? Obviously not, since a culture may or may not provide possibilities for the intelligible use of the expressions appealed to in the examples. This is why the invoking of the task facing Kierkegaard is so instructive. Stanley Cavell has explored the philosophical complexities involved in the task.

Kierkegaard, in the essay Cavell discusses,[5] is faced with the problem of showing those who represent the dominant religious traditions of his day that they had lost an understanding of faith. Cavell says that Kierkegaard's task was different from that of Luther: 'Luther's success was to break the hold of an external authority and put it back into the individual soul, but what happens when *that* authority is broken? Luther's problem was to combat false definitions of religious categories, but Kierkegaard has to provide definition for them from the beginning; Luther could say, "The mass is not a sacrifice, but a promise", and now Kierkegaard's problem is that no one remembers what a promise is, nor has the authority to accept one.'[6] If the matter rested there, however, no philosophical issues would be involved. It would simply be a case of a religious writer regretting that people had forgotten something he would have them remember. It has been suggested that there would be an analogy with what has been said so far if, over time, people came to mean by 'I promise', 'I will if it is convenient'.[7] We might say that people had forgotten what it is to promise, or, at least, one concept of promising. Yet it is a further complexity which introduces the relevant philosophical issues. It has been said, rightly, that

Kierkegaard's situation was even more complex than our descriptions of it so far would suggest. 'Not only was there a forgetfulness present in the careless and loose use of Christian terms, but there were also philosophers and theologians about who were offering new interpretations of Christian terms. The analogy to this would be philosophers coming on the scene to declare that the real and abiding essence of the concept of promise is the intention to do if convenient.'[8] It is the claim of philosophers to be talking of the 'real and abiding essence of the concept' which makes the issue a philosophical one. Were it not for this claim, all we would have is the analysis of two meanings, a noting of a conceptual transformation.

One more complexity needs to be noted: not only is the new analysis said to reveal the *only* meaning that religious beliefs or promises could have, but the new analysis wants to travel in the name of the old, making claims in the name of the new concept which can only be made in terms of the old.

In the two contexts we have noted: that in which an old concept is threatened by a new one which claims to be the only possible meaning, and that in which new concepts make claims which only make sense in the context of the concepts which have been eroded or replaced, the philosopher's task is to point out what possibilities of meaning are being ignored or distorted. Cavell gives an excellent account of the task facing Kierkegaard in this context:

> In this book, Kierkegaard characterizes our age in a few, very specific and often repeated, ways; his task is to provide corrections specific to them . . . . In his first Preface Kierkegaard says he uses the Adler case 'to defend dogmatic concepts', and in the second Preface he claims that from the book one will 'get a clarity about certain dogmatic concepts and an ability to use them' (p. xv). By 'defend dogmatic concepts' he does not mean 'provide a dogmatic backing for them', but rather something like 'defend them as themselves dogmatic'; as, so to speak,

> carrying their own specific religious weight – something, it is implied, theology now fails to do – and this is a matter of coming to see clearly what they mean. So his task is one of providing, or re-providing, their meaning; in a certain sense, giving each its definition. This definition is not to provide some new sense to be attached to a word, with the purpose of better classifying information or outfitting a new theory; it is to clarify what the word does mean, as we use it in our lives – what it means, that is, to anyone with the ability to use it.[9]

It is important to remember, however, that Kierkegaard *does* see himself as confronted by a religious and philosophical task. Difficult though it is, Kierkegaard does think it possible to retell the old truths and present philosophical accounts of them in such a way that his age can hear them again. Given that he is confronted by a task positively conceived of, Cavell's view of Kierkegaard needs to be modified. To say that Kierkegaard started from the beginning does not mean that he started in a vacuum. On the contrary, he was able to speak because he and others had not forgotten what many had forgotten. Again, Kierkegaard himself goes too far in saying that 'the concept of authority has been entirely forgotten in our confused age.'[10] The concept cannot be *entirely* forgotten if Kierkegaard's religious and philosophical tasks are to be as Cavell describes them. Such complete forgetfulness would belong to a time when the old meanings had completely disintegrated. Nevertheless, in depicting the confusion of his age, Kierkegaard is characterising a pervasive estrangement from, and a forgetfulness of, beliefs and concepts which were once dominant in human lives.

Clearly, if philosophers can be confused because of what they do not know in the accounts they give of religious belief, confused about concepts which *they* do not use when not philosophising, it cannot be said that philosophical problems are solved 'by arranging what we have always known'. Here, the confused do not know anything to arrange! Although this is true, it does not involve any necessity to revise what Wittgenstein meant by reflecting on ordinary language in the resolving of philosophical problems. We may think otherwise if we consider the reminders which take the form 'When *we* say . . .' or 'What *we* mean by . . .' as *generalisations*. Cavell has shown elsewhere that they should not be read as such. When the word 'we' is used in such reminders as 'What we mean by . . .' a community of usage is invoked, but *not* necessarily a community to which *everyone* belongs. When we reflect on a religious linguistic use, therefore, we need not be reflecting on a use which we, as individuals, participate in. It follows that the reminders 'When we say . . .' and 'What we mean . . .' are not contradicted or falsified if an individual or group of individuals responds by saying, 'Well, *I* don't' or 'That's not true of us'. All that follows is that the responses show that those who make them are outside the community of usage which has been invoked.[11] Why should Wittgenstein be read as saying that philosophy only asks us to reflect on that which we have already made our own?

We have seen, then, that no revision of what Wittgenstein means by reflection on ordinary language is necessary in order to take account of forgetfulness or distortion concerning concepts in the context of cultural change. Still, in the contexts we have considered so far, religious reminders of what has been forgotten or distorted can still be given. Kierkegaard is a provider. But what is the role of philosophy in giving an account of cultural contexts where, despite confusion being present, there is little confidence that religious reminders of the meaningful can be given? It may be said that this new context marks the difference between the worlds Kierkegaard and Beckett show to us. Beckett, like Kierkegaard, though of course to nothing like the same extent, has some sense of what old stories used to tell. Yet, unlike Kierkegaard, Beckett cannot re-tell the story in such a way that his age can hear it. On the contrary, he seems to be saying that there is no authentic language available in which the story can be our story. The authenticity of Beckett's voice, to a large extent, lies in its expression of this impotence. Yet, even such a situation demands some kind of memory of what it was once possible to say. The memory of meanings no longer pervasive is extremely important, since it is that which enables Beckett to exercise a *via negativa* in relation to the pseudo-substitutes and panaceas which try to fill the void created by the lost meanings. As Cavell says in his essay on Beckett's *Endgame*, 'Nowadays, if you pour the wine of new meanings into old bottles, it is the wine which breaks. And all bottles are old.'[12]

What is the task of philosophy in the kind of context to which Beckett draws our attention? The answer is that it has before it *the task of understanding the character and implications of this context itself*, since they are easily misunderstood. One such misunderstanding would be the assumption that philosophy itself should be able to provide new positive perspectives in the void. The misunderstanding, as we shall see, does not consist in having expectations which, as a matter of fact, will not be fulfilled. The misunderstanding is in the character of the expectations themselves; they involve conceptual confusions. Nothing in Wittgenstein suggests that we should not consider such confusions. We have seen already that Wittgenstein was acutely aware of and interested in the conceptual implications of cultural change. Cavell points out that when Wittgenstein says that 'Philosophy may in no way interfere with the actual use of language; it can in the end only describe it. For it cannot give it any foundation either. It leaves everything as it is',[13] 'There is a frame of mind in which such words may appear as something intolerably confining. Then one will hear Wittgenstein's statement as though it meant . . . that philosophy ought not to change it (in which case Wittgenstein will be accused of an intellectual, even social, conservatism).'[14] We have seen that a similar conservatism has been attributed to those influenced by Wittgenstein in the philosophy of religion. We have also seen, in the first two chapters, why such criticisms are misplaced. Leaving everything where it is involves taking account of cultural turmoil as much as cultural stability. It is the Wittgenstein who is accused of conservatism who said, in 1937: 'Just as people say that the physicists in ancient times found suddenly that what they understood of mathematics was not enough to enable them to master the problem of physics, we might say that the young people of today are suddenly in a situation in which a normal sound understanding is no longer adequate to the queer demands of life. Everything is so confused/bent/ tangled that it would need an exceptional understanding to master it. For, it is no longer enough to be able to play the game well. For over and over again the question is: can this game be played now anyway? What is the right game?'[15]

Yet it is in contexts such as these that the philosopher of religion must endeavour to pursue his reflections in an effort to achieve clarity. There is no way he can avoid the task of producing telling examples. If he wants to show that there is a multiplicity of language-games, that they must be regarded as complete and not as the incomplete parts of a wider system, the force of the example is essential. Yet, unsurprisingly, many, in face of Wittgenstein's examples concerning religion and ritual cannot or will not take them in the ways he wants them to take them. There have been similar reactions to Winch's discussion of witchcraft[16] and to the reflections I tried to offer in*The Concept of Prayer.*

In a further discussion of the problems involved in understanding the practices of another culture, Winch makes a point which our observations in this chapter give us every reason to concur with, namely, that we cannot assume that our language – the English language – is capable, without extension, of translating the basic concepts of these languages. Our failure to see the point of certain practices in people's lives may be due to the pointlessness of our own in certain respects.[17] As we saw in the last chapter,[18] it will not do to say, as Wittgenstein did once, that the language we possess already gives us a principle by means of which possibilities of meaning in cultures other than our own can be ordered. Neither will it do to say with Chesterton that all a student of folk-lore has to do in face of these examples is 'to look at them from the inside, and ask himself how he would begin a story',[19] for why should the way *he* would order such a story be the principle which governs all possibilities, all eventualities?

Faced, then, with religious practices from his own or other cultures, a philosopher may find difficulty in the presentation of his reflections via examples. The obstacles with which he is faced may be partly aesthetic, akin to the difficulty of getting someone to see why one development of a theme is more appropriate than another. The obstacles may be moral or psychological – a person may be unable to bring himself to think in a certain way. The obstacles may be philosophical – a person may not see the implications of the language he himself uses quite naturally when not philosophising. In all these cases, an offered example will prove unacceptable; it will not be taken in the way one intended it to be taken. Speaking of the immortality of the soul, Wittgenstein says, 'It might seem as though, if we asked such a question as "Does Lewy really mean what so and so means when he says so-and-so is alive?" – it might seem as though there were two sharply divided cases, one in which he would say that he didn't mean it literally. I want to say this is not so. There will be cases where we will differ, and where it won't be a question at all of more or less knowledge, so that we can come together.'[20] Examples will be offered in discussion, but they will not hit the mark. At this point, discussion itself may well come to a full stop. Still, it may be said that this eventuality, given the arguments of the last and the present chapter, should not be altogether surprising.

Yet we have had to recognise the presence of further complexities. In speaking of philosophical obstacles to the reception of conceptual reminders, I said that a person may not see the implications of the language he is using when not philosophising. Unfortunately, as we have seen, the matter does not rest there. The philosophical observations may themselves have a feed-back into the language which is misunderstood, so that the philosophical confusions themselves become a substantive part of what is believed. This has happened again and again in the philosophy of religion. Religion itself becomes infected with bad philosophical accounts of itself, so that it becomes difficult sometimes to say where philosophy or religious belief begin or end. Familiarity with our own culture need be no safeguard in this respect. On the contrary, Chesterton brings out well how, in some cases, the strangeness of an example can be an advantage (*pace* Winch) whereas its cultural proximity may be a disadvantage. 'Things that may well be familiar as long as familiarity breeds affection', he argues, 'had much better become unfamiliar when familiarity breeds contempt'.[21] Speaking as a Roman Catholic, Chesterton says, '. . . the next best thing to being really inside Christendom is to be really outside it'.[22] In this latter context there is still the possibility of approaching the beliefs with the wonder and strangeness of a child. What is fatal, Chesterton claims, is a kind of half-way position characterised by rationalism and scientism. 'They suggest everywhere the grey gradations of twilight, because they believe it is the twilight of the gods. I propose to maintain that whether or no it is the twilight of the gods, it is not the daylight of men'.[23]

Chesterton had in mind, of course, writers who thought they could, by their explanations, explain religion away. But what of philosophical aberrations which feed, not a belief in the twilight of the gods, but a belief that light is being thrown on what it means to believe in God or to assert his existence? What happens then? As we shall see in the next chapter, one thing that happens is that voices are raised against religion accusing it of distorting what we know in such a way that it forfeits the right to be taken seriously. The only serious attention religion deserves becomes that which we expend in opposing vulgarities which threaten common decency.

4 The Challenge of What We Know: The Problem of Evil

In the last chapter we noted the complexity of the philosophical task with which Kierkegaard was faced. He believed that there had been a widespread forgetfulness of the meaning of certain fundamental religious concepts. His task, it seemed, was simply to provide reminders of the meanings which had been forgotten. Here, however, certain further facts complicated his task, facts to do with much philosophical and theological activity of his time. 'Not only was there a forgetfulness present in the careless and loose use of Christian terms, but there were also philosophers and theologians about who were offering new interpretations of Christian terms. The analogy to this would be philosophers coming on the scene to declare that the real and abiding essence of the concept of promise is the intention to do if convenient.'[1] Here, in the ethical case, the philosophical analysis would itself infect the old concept of a promise, changing it substantively. If such influence were successful, one would have to conclude that this is what promising had now become. Before that stage is reached, people who remember the old concept of a promise will continue to protest that in saying what a promise *must* be, the new analysis distorts what they know. In that sense, what they know is a challenge to the new analysis.

A similar situation faces us in contemporary philosophy of religion, although it must be said that the distorting philosophical analyses are not particularly new. Here, too, philosophers try to state what religious responses *must* be in ways which take us away from other possibilities of religious belief, and in ways which distort what we know of the realities of human life.

In the first chapter, in responding to the third and fourth theses attributed to philosophers of religion influenced by Wittgenstein, namely, that whatever is called religious determines what is and what is not meaningful in religion, and that religion cannot be criticised, I said: '. . . the connections between religious beliefs' and what we know 'must not be fantastic . . . whether the connections are fantastic is decided by criteria which are not in dispute'.[2] We have seen that this claim for agreement in criteria can be too optimistic. Nevertheless, in some areas, there will be a large measure of agreement on certain facts, and if what is offered in the name of religion ignores these, then, what we all know will constitute a formidable challenge to what is offered. As I said in the first chapter, 'For example, some religious believers may try to explain away the reality of suffering, or try to say that all suffering has some point. When they speak like this, one may accuse them of not taking suffering seriously.'[3] I said that this suggestion would be given a fuller treatment in this chapter.

It is not surprising that the most frequent form of the accusation that religion obscures or distorts the realities of human life is found as a reaction to what various religious apologists have had to say about human suffering. Disputes surrounding the topic have come to be known as the problem of evil. Here, in the treatment of what religion has to say in face of evil, we often have examples of how philosophy can obscure rather than clarify realities for us.

Kierkegaard once depicted a source of confusion in philosophy as thoroughly investigating details of a road one should not have turned into in the first place.[4] Such confusion, it seems to me, can be found in the ways in which many philosophers and theologians insist on the way in which belief in God is supposed to make sense of the evils in the world. According to them, there *must* be some good to be found in evil, however extreme, a good which has been designed by God, the Great Architect, according to whose plans we live out our lives. In this chapter, I shall consider some details of the road down which such philosophers and theologians would have us travel. On their own terms they ask us to submit the ways in which they talk to a compatibility test: what they say of the Great Architect must fit in with what we know of the high-ways and by-ways of human life. If it can be shown that what we are asked to think about these roads and the people who live there distorts what we know or goes beyond the limits of what we are prepared to think, this in itself would be a reason against the insistence on extrapolating possibilities of divine policy from such dubious facts. The observations of the chapter will, therefore, be negative in the main; an attempt will be made to show why we do not have to go down a certain road – a road which illustrates how philosophy can obscure religious realities and much else besides.

On our travels, I shall take some arguments by Richard Swinburne as an example of the tendencies I want to oppose.[5] His terms of reference for the journey are well known: it is to seek an answer to the question of how evils are compatible with the existence of an omnipotent, omniscient, all-good God. Swinburne is a theodicist, someone who seeks to answer this question by justifying God's ways to men, by showing us why things are as they are and, in particular, why that which appears to be evil to us, has been sent or created by God for the general good of mankind: a little evil does no one any harm and even the greatest evil, on closer examination, turns out to be worth the price.

Swinburne's first observation is that all men are guilty of some wrong actions. Could men have been naturally good? That is a logical and not a factual question. Does the supposition make sense? If not, it makes no sense either to blame God for not creating perfect human beings. Swinburne holds that 'it is not logically possible to create humanly free agents such that necessarily they do not do morally evil actions.'[6] Let us ask first whether we could have a world in which men always make the right decisions and where no actual evil exists. If we are retaining, as this talk may be doing, a world such as ours, where deliberations and temptations are what we know them to be, these assumptions soon run into conceptual difficulties. Consider the following course of argument: someone may say that acquiring moral conceptions entails the existence of actual evil in the world. For example, a child may be taught to condemn selfishness by being restrained from performing a selfish action. His arm may be pulled back as he reaches for a third cream bun. Moral consideration, it may be said, develops partly by commenting on what is actually happening. To this it may be retorted that disdain of evil could be taught by means of hypothetical inference without actual evils taking place.[7] For example, a child may be told that if human beings were killed as animals are killed that would be a bad thing. Putting this suggestion aside for a moment, how could evil thoughts be eliminated? Some may think that the possibility of saints whose lives are characterised by spontaneous virtues constitutes an answer to this question. Their generosity of spirit may be such that they do not entertain such thoughts. This reply, however, does not work. The impressiveness of saints cannot be explained by an attempt to isolate their characteristics in this way. We are impressed by the generosity of spirit which saints may possess, precisely because they possess it in a world where it is all too easy to think otherwise of human beings. These observations about the saints admit of wider application. Generosity, kindness, loyalty, truth, etc., do get their identity in a world where meanness, cruelty, disloyalty and lies are also possible. We see the importance of virtues, not in face of apparent or possible evils, but in face of actual evils. Swinburne himself rejects the possibility of a world where God has seen to it that people only seem to be harmed, since God would be guilty of deception if this were the case. The objection, however, is logical, not moral. When we think we ought to be generous, is it in face of apparent need or real need? How could we know the difference? The point is that we cannot, according to the argument. But this 'cannot' is unintelligible, for no distinction between what can and cannot be known exists to give it any import. God, on this argument, suffers the same fate as Descartes's malignant demon. If we now look again at the question, could there be a world where men are naturally good? we can see, for reasons already given, that such a world could not contain people we would call good. Even so, would a world of such people, whatever we call them, be a better world than the world we know? I have no idea how to answer this question.

Swinburne doubts whether the notion of the best of all logically possible worlds makes sense, but even if it did, he cannot see how God could have any obligation to create it. He does, however, think it makes sense to compare a universe without actual evil, a finished universe, with our own, a half-finished universe. Swinburne says, 'While not wishing to deny the goodness of a universe of the first kind, I suggest that to create a universe of the (other) kind would be no bad thing, for it gives to creatures the privilege of making their own universe.'[8] Putting aside the dubious character of this privilege for the moment, I take it that Swinburne would also say that God could have no obligation to create such a universe. If Swinburne's conception of God were allowed, and that, as we shall see, is to allow a great deal, what can be made of Swinburne's defence of him? Swinburne asks, '. . . to whom could he be doing an injustice if he did not?'[9] The suggestion seems to be that God has no obligation to create a world of any particular kind, since prior to his act of creation, there are no people to harm! But this is no defence. If God were asked why he created such a world for people to live in instead of a better one, and should his answer be, 'They wouldn't know the difference', an appropriate reply, even if it could not be uttered, would be, 'No, but you did!'

Having raised some difficulties concerning the possibility of a world of naturally good men which contains no actual evil and Swinburne's claim that God could not have an obligation to create the best of all possible worlds if that notion made sense, new difficulties arise in the light of Swinburne's further observations. His strategy is placed in the context of the free-will defence, a defence 'which must claim that it is a good thing that there exist free agents with the power and opportunity of choosing between morally good and morally evil actions, agents with sufficient moral discrimination to have some idea of the difference and some (though not overwhelming) temptation to do other than the morally good'.[10] Objections have been made to this defence by philosophers who ask why God has not ensured or seen to it that men, as a result of their free deliberation, always make the right decisions. Swinburne says that God has not done this because it would be an imposition of character on man and therefore morally wrong. My difficulty is that I have the prior problem of not knowing what it means to speak of God either ensuring or not ensuring, seeing to it or not seeing to it, where the development of human character is concerned. My difficulties can be discussed in two contexts: first, the difficulty of the metaphysical level at which the 'ensuring' or 'seeing to it' is supposed to take place, and second, the difficulty of knowing what it would be to see to or ensure the formation of human character.

First, then, the question of the metaphysical character of God's ensuring that human beings have such-and-such characters. There is no difficulty in locating natural events or intentional acts which have influenced a person's character in specific ways. But here I can say that there may or may not have been such effects, or that some people were affected and others not or that different people were affected in different ways. Even if we say that such-and-such an event or action must have an effect of a specifiable kind, there is still a question of how such an effect is taken up into the rest of a person's life. If I want to speak of 'ensuring' or 'seeing to it' that a person exhibits a certain 'character', then I would think of something akin to post-hypnotic suggestion. Here, although the person so influenced 'obeys the command' and 'gives reasons' for his conduct, we do not accept such behaviour without reservation as an instance of what we would call obeying a command or giving reasons. There are features of his behaviour which lead us to detect rationalisation. Of course, on a given occasion, one may be taken in. A man may exhibit anger as the result of a suggestion made to him while under hypnosis in a situation where anger would have been a natural response in any case. The point to stress is not that the seeing to it or the ensuring is always detected, but that we know what it means to speak of detecting it. Add to this the possibility of our having independent knowledge of the hypnosis in the first place. Such direct knowledge is not given to us in God's case, and so we are trying to contemplate what God may or may not have done on the basis of what we already know. My difficulty is to find a discernible difference in human affairs which would confirm or refute these speculations. Those who think it makes sense to speak of God ensuring that men, after free deliberation, always make the right decisions, do not want to think of God as the divine hypnotist since (a) that is not the kind of behaviour God is said to ensure and (b) God's ensuring is not something we can clearly discern as sometimes present and sometimes absent in human affairs, but is that which ensures that human affairs are what they are in the first place. My difficulty, I suppose, concerns the intelligibility of thinking of creation as an act of ensuring or seeing to things that we know, different only in the resources available and the scale of operation.

Second, I find difficulty in knowing what it means to speak of someone ensuring or seeing to it that human characters are of such-and-such a kind. Swinburne does not find this difficult to imagine. He simply thinks it would be a bad thing for God to do, just as it would be a bad thing for parents to do:

> The creator could help agents towards doing right actions by making these reasons more effective causally; that is, he could make agents so that by nature they were inclined (though not perhaps compelled) to pursue what is good. But this would be to impose a moral character on agents, to give them wide general purposes which they naturally pursue, to make them naturally altruistic, tenacious of purpose, or strong willed. However to impose a character

> on creatures might well seem to take away from creatures the privilege of developing their own characters and those of their fellows. We tend to think that parents who try too forcibly to impose a character, however good a character, on their children, are less than perfect parents.[11]

Someone might well argue from the same facts to the opposite conclusion. A parent who wants to ensure or see to it that his child has one sort of character rather than another, it may be said, is not necessarily interfering with the freedom of the child. If we do not regard such measures as an interference with freedom, despite our ignorance and all the mistakes we make, why should a logical or moral limit be drawn on God, who is not ignorant nor liable to error, seeing to it that human beings freely develop in the right way?[12] I do not want to enter the dispute over whether either programme for parental attitudes is right or wrong, since my difficulties over the intelligibility of the programme remain.[13] I am not denying that measures taken by parents may influence the development of their children in the way hoped for by the parents. I deliberately speak in the subjunctive mood and speak of hope, since I think it important to distinguish between the retrospective judgement 'I influenced the development of my child's character' or 'I did what I could' with the claim, 'I ensured or saw to it that my child's character developed in a certain way'. Measures taken in hope recognise that such measures are taken in contexts where a good deal is outside the control of the agent. A wise parent may recognise that this does not simply happen to be true. He would not know what it would mean if someone wanted to talk of parental influence on development of character in any other way. Greater control would recall visions of post-hypnotic behaviour, something we would not include in developments of character at all. Thus the wise parent may say, 'I thank my lucky stars that I was able to help the development of my child's character' or 'I thank God that I was able to help my child'. These references to God or lucky stars, here, are not references to those agents who *did* ensure the outcome. On the contrary, these utterances are themselves reactions to the fact that what is contingent, in the hands of God, we might say, has gone in a certain way. It is ironic that the debate about whether God should or should not have seen to the development of human characters, uproots the language of things being in God's hands from one of its natural contexts, a context which gets much of its force from the fact that talk of ensuring or seeing to it that outcomes are of one sort or another has no place in it.

The consideration of Swinburne's treatment of the question whether men could have been naturally good and whether God could have seen to it that men developed freely in this direction centred on the question of the intelligibility of what Swinburne asks us to imagine. I want now to consider the ways in which he thinks we must think of God in face of more specific evils he has observed. This shift of attention corresponds to the first two moral principles of the anti-theodicist which Swinburne wants to attack. So far he would claim to have disposed of the principle 'that a creator able to do so ought to create only creatures such that necessarily they do not do evil actions'.[14] He wants now to consider the modified second principle, namely, 'that a creator able to do so ought always to ensure that any creature whom he creates does not cause passive evils, or at any rate passive evils which hurt creatures other than himself'.[15] Swinburne's general theodicist strategy within which he attempts to show the implausibility of this principle is 'that it is not morally wrong for God to create or permit the various evils, normally on the grounds that doing so is providing the logically necessary conditions of greater goods'.[16] What is the greater good which justifies the harm that we do to others? Swinburne replies,

> A world in which no one except the agent was affected by his evil actions might be a world in which men had freedom but it would not be a world in which men had responsibility . . . . So then the theodicist objects . . . on the grounds that the price of possible passive evils for other creatures is a price worth paying for agents to have great responsibilities

for each other. It is a price which (logically) must be paid if they are to have these responsibilities.[17]

Swinburne's analysis is not an analysis of what moral responsibility must be. On the contrary it is an analysis of pseudo-responsibility; it involves a vulgarisation of the concept. From the truth that we could not feel responsible unless we were responsible to someone or for something, it does not follow that someone or something should be regarded as opportunities for us to feel responsible. If we remind someone of his responsibilities, we are directing his attention to concerns other than himself. Swinburne's analysis makes these concerns the servants of that self. Compare: 'He recognises the importance of his job' with 'His job makes him feel important'. Similarly, instead of sometimes feeling responsible for or a responsibility towards the affliction of others, Swinburne's analysis would have us look on those afflictions as opportunities for feeling responsible. It is as if the parable of the Good Samaritan were thought to show that unlike the priest and the levite, the Samaritan did not pass by an opportunity of feeling responsible! Nor does it matter if we say that what God provides is not an opportunity for *feeling* responsible, but an opportunity for *being* responsible. The Good Samaritan would be no less objectionable if he regarded the man who had fallen among thieves as an opportunity to be responsible than if he regarded him as an opportunity to feel responsible. The objection has to do with regarding the victim as an *opportunity* for one in this way.

What if someone suggests that viewing people as opportunities, in the context of a theodicy, is an attitude which belongs to God, and not to men, and that therefore my criticisms are misdirected? Even if this were true, it would have the unfortunate consequence, in the light of my previous criticisms, of ascribing to God a moral description which would make him morally inferior to his creatures. He would see men as opportunities, in the sense described, but his creatures would not. Yet, as a matter of fact, in entertaining theodicies, one does think of God and of the evil which occurs in life in this way.

Even if the notion of responsibility had not been vulgarised in Swinburne's analysis, it would not follow that a responsible reaction justifies the evil or suffering which occasion it. This has been well expressed by W. Somerset Maugham:

> It may be that courage and sympathy are excellent and that they could not come into existence without danger and suffering. It is hard to see how the Victoria Cross that rewards the soldier who has risked his life to save a blinded man is going to solace *him* for the loss of his sight. To give alms shows charity, and charity is a virtue, but does *that* good compensate for the evil of the cripple whose poverty has called it forth?[18]

Let us go further down Swinburne's road. He has noticed already that men intentionally bring evil to others, but now he also notices that there is quite a lot of evil around. Therefore he feels that a third moral principle advanced by the anti-theodicist needs answering, namely, 'that a creator able to do so ought to ensure that any creature whom he creates does not cause passive evils as many and as evil as those in our world'.[19] God may have set a moral obstacle race for mankind, but are the obstacles too difficult? A defender of the third moral principle 'says that in our world freedom and responsiblity have gone too far – produced too much physical and mental hurt. God might well tolerate a boy hitting his younger brother, but not Belsen'.[20] Swinburne admits that this would be a telling criticism if true, but as he looks around him he does not believe it is true. On the contrary, Swinburne believes that God has created a world where the men are sorted out from the boys. It means 'that the creator must create them immature, and allow them gradually to take decisions which affect the sort of beings they will be'.[21] This is why Swinburne calls our world 'a half-finished universe'. The words are well-chosen, since the picture is of a finishing-school with God as the benevolent headmaster setting the tests. But does Swinburne's God pass the test of benevolence? It is hard to see that he does when we hear Swinburne's argument to show that in allowing evil God has not gone too far.

> There are limits to the amount and degree of evil which is possible in our world. Thus there are limits to the amount of pain which a person can suffer – persons only live in our world so many years and the amount which they can suffer at any given time (if mental goings-on are in any way correlated with bodily ones) is limited by their physiology . . . . So the theodicist can certainly claim that a good God stops too much suffering – it is just that he and his opponent draw the line in different places.[22]

Can the theodicist make such a claim on the basis of Swinburne's argument? I think not. There is an unwarrantable transition in the argument from talk of the world to talk about human beings, and, more importantly, from conceivable limits to actual limits. Of course, for any evils in the world we mention, more can be conceived of, but this is neither here nor there as far as the question of whether human beings are visited with greater afflictions than they can bear is concerned. Swinburne argues that since any human being can stand only so much suffering and we can conceive of more, it follows that God has not produced unlimited suffering and therefore has not gone too far. But, clearly, he has produced too much suffering for that human being and has gone too far for him. Such questions cannot be answered in an abstract or global way. What constitutes a limit or going too far for one person may not do so for another. In order to judge whether a human being has suffered more than he can bear, we need to refer to actual limits, not conceivable limits. By judging actual limits as if they were the limits of the conceivable, Swinburne could deny that even a person's death could count as going too far in his case. 'After all,' he might say, 'he could have died a worse death'! I find this whole defence rather perverse. God's finishing-school is one where everyone is finished in one sense or another. Either they are well-finished, educated to maturity by their experience in the moral obstacle race, or they are finished off completely by it. If the finishing-off were done by someone who was solely the bringer of death, then, in certain circumstances, he would be described as the bringer of welcome release. But this is not true of Swinburne's God. Since the bringer of death is also the bringer of afflictions, he who devised the whole fiendish obstacle race, one cannot even attribute to him the compassion with which a dog may be put out of his misery. On the contrary, as each candidate fails to make the grade, it is surely more appropriate to say with Hardy that thus God ended his play. Let us hurry from this scene.

Swinburne, of course, would object to this reaction. He would argue that in considering particular examples we *always* need more information. We cannot rule out *a priori* that some point to evil could emerge even in the most horrific cases. Yet, if one cannot rule out *a priori* the possibility of something turning up, neither can one rule out *a priori* the possibility that nothing will turn up. Swinburne sometimes seems to suggest that we can *never* be sure that people have reached the limits of pointless suffering. But this claim is a metaphysical one and is not informative in any way. Nothing counts for or against it; it is an example of language idling. Swinburne's claim that we just do not know whether people had to give in to the forces operating on them until philosophers and scientists have solved the free-will problem is an incredible claim. Our knowledge of people who have been crushed by circumstances in their lives, people who had more than they could bear, does not wait on philosophy and science.

My reaction in turning away from some of the things Swinburne says may be misunderstood. It may be taken for evasion. It may seem as if, when I present an example of pointless suffering, and Swinburne gives it a point, I ignore his challenge by producing another example. This misconceives why I try to get Swinburne to move on. What I am trying to get him to see is that, sometimes, searching for a point to the evil is not to make matters better, but to make matters worse. Of course, I am not saying that a consideration of consequences is never morally desirable. What I am saying is that *sometimes* a readiness to do so is a sign of corruption. The same is true of being open-minded.

As he goes further down his road, Swinburne thinks that the possibility of evil must be justified in terms of the opportunities for noble action it provides:

> . . . given a creator, then, without an immoral act on his part, for acts of courage, compassion etc. to be acts open to men to perform, there have to be various evils. Evils give men the opportunity to perform those acts which show men at their best. A world without evils would be a world in which men could show no forgiveness, no compassion, no self-sacrifice. And men without that opportunity are deprived of the opportunity to show themselves at their noblest. For this reason God might well allow some of his creatures to perform evil acts with passive evils as consequences, since these provide the opportunity for especially noble acts.[23]

This argument ignores a great deal, its main defect being its one-sided optimism. Why should evil beget good? One cannot show forgiveness without something to forgive, but that something may destroy or prompt savage reactions. In a man's own life natural evils such as illness or social evils such as poverty may debase and destroy him. Swinburne says:

> Pain normally occurs when something goes wrong with the working of our body which is going to lead to further limitation on the purposes which we can achieve; and the pain ends when the body is repaired. The existence of the pain spurs the sufferer, and others through the sympathetic suffering which arises when they learn of the sufferer's pain, to do something about the bodily malfunctioning. Yet giving men such feelings which they are inclined to end involves the imposition of no character.[24]

Swinburne is faced with formidable contrary testimony often expressed in art or from recollection of experience. Here are some of Settembrini's comments to Hans Castorp in Thomas Mann's *The Magic Mountain*:

> You said that the sight of dullness and disease going hand in hand must be the most melancholy in life. I grant you, I grant you that. I too prefer an intelligent ailing person to a consumptive idiot. But I take issue where you regard the combination of disease with dullness as a sort of aesthetic inconsistency, an error in taste on the part of nature, a 'dilemma for the human feelings', as you were pleased to express yourself. When you professed to regard disease as something so refined, so – what did you call it? – possessing a 'certain dignity' – that it doesn't 'go with' stupidity. That was the expression you used. Well, I say no! Disease has nothing refined about it, nothing dignified. Such a conception is in itself pathological, or at least tends in that direction . . . . Do not, for heaven's sake, speak to me of the ennobling effects of physical suffering! A soul without a body is as inhuman and horrible as a body without a soul – though the latter is the rule and the former the exception. It is the body, as a rule, which flourishes exceedingly, which draws everything to itself, which usurps the predominant place and lives repulsively emancipated from the soul. A human being who is first of all an invalid is *all* body; therein lies his inhumanity and his debasement. In most cases he is little better than a carcass.[25]

Here too are W. Somerset Maugham's recollections of what he saw in hospital wards as he trained for the medical profession:

> At that time (a time to most people of sufficient ease, when peace seemed certain and prosperity secure) there was a school of writers who enlarged upon the moral value of suffering. They claimed that it was salutary. They claimed that it increased sympathy and enhanced the sensibilities. They claimed that it opened to the spirit new awareness of beauty and enables it to get into touch with the mystical kingdom of God. They claimed that it strengthened the character, purified it from its human grossness, and brought to him who did not avoid but sought it a more

> perfect happiness . . . I set down in my note-books, not once or twice, but in a dozen places, the facts that I had seen. I knew that suffering did not ennoble; it degraded. It made men selfish, mean, petty, and suspicious. It absorbed them in small things. It did not make them more than men; it made them less than men; and I wrote ferociously that we learn resignation not by our own suffering, but by the suffering of others.[26]

Not only need evil not occasion goodness, but goodness itself may occasion evils. Swinburne does not consider these possibilities. The depth of a man's love may lead him to kill his wife's lover or to be destroyed when the object of his love is lost to him. A man whose love was mediocre would not have done either of these things. Love has as much to do with the terrible as with the wonderful. The presence of goodness in some may be the cause of hatred in others. Budd's goodness is more than Claggart can bear and it is the very possibility that deep love may be a reality which Iago cannot admit into his dark soul.

On his travels, Swinburne has seen how human beings intervene from time to time to help each other in their troubles. Sometimes, when fortunate, they can prevent those troubles occurring, and they often try to prevent things getting worse. He realises then that he *has* to answer the question why his God does not intervene in circumstances where mere mortals would not hesitate. His answers are not encouraging. They amount to saying that just as parents know more than their children and are often right not to act even when their offspring beg them to do so, so God, the Father of us all, knowing more than we know, refrains from acting despite the cries of the afflicted. Here is a sample:

> Hence a God who sees far more clearly than we do the consequences of quarrels may have duties very different from ours with respect to particular such quarrels. He may know that the suffering that A will cause B is not nearly as

> great as B's screams may suggest to us and will provide (unknown to us) an opportunity to C to help B recover and will thus give C a deep responsibility which he would not otherwise have.[27]

I have commented already on the character of such a sense of responsibility, and that is not my purpose now. It is true that considering a matter further is sometimes a sign of reasonableness and maturity. But this cannot be stated absolutely, since, at other times, readiness to be open-minded about such matters is a sign of a corrupt mind. There are screams and screams, and to ask of what use are the screams of the innocent, as Swinburne's defence would have us do, is to embark on a speculation we should not even contemplate. We have our reasons, final human reasons, for putting a moral full-stop at many places.[28] If God has other reasons, they are his reasons, not ours, and they do not overrule them. That is why, should he ask us to consider them, we, along with Ivan Karamazov, respectfully, or not so respectfully, return him the ticket. So when Swinburne says 'The argument must go on with regard to particular cases . . . . The exhibition of consequences is a long process, and it takes time to convince an opponent even if he is prepared to be rational, more time than is available in this paper', [29] one must not be misled by the apparent reasonableness. Often, when the invitation to consider consequences is made, the appropriate reply is 'Get thee behind me, Satan!' And if there is a 'higher' form of reasoning among God and his angels, where such matters are open for compromise and calculation, then so much the worse for God and his angels. If they reason in this way in the heavenly places, we can say with Wallace Stevens, 'Alas that they should wear our colours there'.

Swinburne notices that there are natural and mental evils which are not the result of intentional actions. How are these to be justified? He claims that our answer must be that pains give men additional reasons for changing states of affairs without imposing a character on them.

> An itch causally inclines a man to do whatever will cause the itch to cease, e.g. scratch, and provides a reason for doing that action. Its causal inference is quite independent of the agent – saint or sinner, strong-willed or weak-willed will all be strongly inclined to get rid of their pains (though some may learn to resist the inclination). Hence a creator who wished to give agents some inclination to improve the world without giving them a character, a wide set of general purposes which they naturally pursue, would tie some of the imperfections of the world to physical or mental evils.[30]

This is a strange argument. In so far as these causal effects become reasons for a man, one will have to take account of the man's character to appreciate what role the reason plays in his life, how it connects up with other considerations he thinks important. Even if the causal influence of certain pains is undeniable, one cannot, as we have seen already, argue for an easy transition between this recognition and its becoming a reason for working towards improvement. The character of the transition, or whether there is one at all, cannot be wholly determined without reference to the character of the person concerned. Kierkegaard provides a good example of what I mean in the case of the calculating rake: 'Indeed, fear of the body's infirmities has taught the voluptuary to observe moderation in debauchery . . . but it has never made him chaste.'[31] Furthermore, if a man's life were governed by the calculation of the acquiring or avoiding of such pains in relation to the policy of moral or immoral conduct, surely the character at work would be a servile one.[32]

Similar conclusions can be drawn regarding Swinburne's remarks on mental evils. He says,

> Many mental evils too are caused by things going wrong in a man's life or in the life of his fellows and often serve as a spur to a man to put things right, either to put right the cause of the particular mental evil or to put similar things right. A man's feeling of frustration at the failure of his plans spurs him either to fulfil those plans despite their

> initial failure or to curtail his ambitions. A man's sadness at the failure of the plans of his child will incline him to help the child more in the future. A man's grief at the absence of a loved one inclines him to do whatever will get the loved one back. As with physical pain, the spur inclines a man to do what is right but does so without imposing a character – without, say, making a man responsive to duty, or strong-willed.[33]

We have seen already that Swinburne's analysis does not work in the case of physical pain, save in simple, straightforward cases. Yet one will not get very far by suggesting that mental evils stand to behaviour as toothache stands to the search for a remedy. Karenin was in mental anguish at the loss of Anna to Vronsky. He was certainly frustrated at the failure of his plans. He was spurred on to fulfil those plans. Nevertheless, it would be absurd to think that an account could be given of his anguish or frustration without introducing considerations of character, considerations internally related to the nature of his subsequent behaviour.

Having travelled with Swinburne to the end of the road he has chosen to go down, noting various ills and misfortunes to which human beings are subject, we are now in a position to summarise the answer to the problem of evil which he brings before us: there are doubts as to whether it makes sense to imagine men who are naturally good without actual evils in the world. It is equally doubtful to say that God ought to have seen to it that men freely reach the right decision. Even if the notion of the best of all logically possible worlds made sense, God would have no obligation to create such a world, for whom would he harm if he did not? There are good reasons for saying that the various ills in the world are compatible with the existence of an omnipotent, omniscient, all-good God. Such evils as we bring on others give us the opportunity of feeling or being responsible, and that is a good thing. After all, such evils are not unlimited, since there is a limit to what anyone can stand. Evils give us the opportunity to be seen at our best in reacting to them. God does not intervene to prevent evil when any decent man would, because he has a wider knowledge of the situations in which the evils occur. In order to prompt us in the right direction without imposing characters on us, God has seen to it that physical and mental evils are linked to things going wrong. According to Swinburne, this is how we *must* think if we are to answer the problem of evil.

Looking back at the details of his case, Swinburne says that 'a morally sensitive anti-theodicist might well in principle accept some of the above arguments'.[34] This conclusion is a somewhat embarrassing one since it is clear from my comments that one of the strongest criticisms available to the anti-theodicist would be the moral insensitivity of the theodicist's case. There is an example in Billie Holiday's autobiography which combines many of the circumstances to which Swinburne calls our attention, but which also sums up the fragility of his optimistic analyses. She tells of a well-known jazz personality who was a drug addict:

> I can tell you about a big-name performer who had a habit and a bad one. There were times when he had it licked. And other times it licked him. It went around that way for years. He was well known, like me, which makes it worse. He had bookings to make, contracts to fulfil. In the middle of one engagement he was about to crack up and go crazy because he had run out of stuff. There was no way in God's world that he could kick cold turkey and make three shows a day. There wasn't a doctor in town who would be seen looking at him. His wife got so scared he'd kill himself that she tried to help him the only way she knew – by risking her own neck and trying to get him what he needed. She went out in the street like a pigeon, begging everyone she knew for help. Finally she found someone who sold her some stuff for an arm and a leg. It was just her luck to be carrying it back to her old man when she was arrested.
>
> She was as innocent and clean as the day she was born.

> But she knew that if she tried to tell that to the cops it would only make her a 'pusher' under the law, liable for a good long time in jail. She thought if she told them she was a user, and took some of the stuff in her pocket to prove it, they might believe her, feel sorry for her, go easy on her. And she could protect her man. So that's what she did. She used junk for the first time to prove to the law she wasn't a pusher. And that's the way she got hooked. She's rotting in jail right now. Yes siree bob, life is just a bowl of cherries.[35]

Later, Billie Holiday sums up her own attitude: 'If you expect nothing but trouble, maybe a few happy days will turn up. If you expect happy days, look out.'[36]

In replying to Swinburne's arguments I have chosen in the main to comment on his reading of the fortunes and misfortunes of human life, a reading which is to serve in the construction of a theodicy. Theodicies such as Swinburne's are marked by their order, optimism and progress. If we want to appreciate why there is no necessity for us to turn down the road on which Swinburne chooses to travel this, above all, is what has to be put aside. Throughout Swinburne's paper, the main emphasis, with only an occasional hint of difficulties, is on the world as a God-given setting in which human beings can exercise rational choices which determine the kind of people they are to become. This is neither the world I know, nor the world Swinburne lives in. Ours is a world where disasters of natural and moral kinds can strike without rhyme or reason, where, if much can be done to influence character, much over which we have no control can also have such an influence. Character has as much, and probably more, to do with reacting to the unavoidable, as with choosing between possible alternatives. Commenting on a similar order, progress and optimism to Swinburne's in twentieth-century moral philosophy, I had reason to quote Hardy's comments on the limits which life placed on Tess's endeavours:

> Nature does not often say 'See!' to her poor creature at a time when seeing can lead to happy doing; or reply 'Here!'

> to a body's cry of 'Where?' till the hide-and-seek has become an irksome, outworn game. We may wonder whether at the acme and summit of the human progress these anachronisms will be corrected by a finer intuition, a closer interaction of the social machinery than that which now jolts us round and along; but such completeness is not to be prophesied, or even conceived as possible.[37]

And yet, even such poor creatures are heard to talk to God. John Hick finds this hard to believe since, for him, to turn away from theodicies is to turn away from God. He is convinced that that is at the root of the differences between Swinburne and myself – Swinburne believes in God and I do not. Needless to say, the philosophical issues I have raised do not concern our personal beliefs. Hick thinks I would object to someone saying that he believed in 'the existence of an all-powerful and limitlessly loving God'.[38] Anyone who has this belief believes, according to Hick, 'that in addition to all the many human consciousnesses there is another consciousness which is the consciousness of God'.[39] That I should certainly contest. I contest it as a philosopher's gloss on the nature of religious belief. For Hick, my views entail atheism. He says that my 'fundamental objection to theodicies is the wholesale one that since there is no *theos* there can be no theodicy'.[40] But, on the contrary, my claim is that the urge to construct theodicies is itself the result of a confused view of what the relation between the will of God and the lives of men and women must be.

Hick claims that for me 'the "existence of God" consists in man's use – his spontaneous and committed use – of theistic language'.[41] These words are puzzling. Clearly, a man's commitment to God shows itself in the language he uses, not only about God, but about the world and in his general behaviour. That he is able to have such a commitment depends on there being a shared language and shared practices in which he can partake. But if Hick is saying that for me commitment to God *means* commitment to language, the results would be obviously absurd. I do not think 'I believe in the language almighty' would strike a responsive chord in many and I certainly would not recognise it as an account of religious belief.

The puzzle deepens when Hick presents philosophers with the exclusive choice of thinking of God either as an additional consciousness or as a thought in men's minds. I may think about sticks and stones. I must master certain techniques of reference and identity in doing so. But when I think about sticks and stones, I do not think that sticks and stones are mere thoughts in my mind. Even when the empiricists said that bodies were collections of ideas, they wanted to distinguish between perceiving a dagger and the dagger which is a mere thought in my mind. In mathematical reasoning we do not find notions of reference comparable to those operative in our talk of physical objects, and yet when we think of mathematical operations we do not think they are thoughts in our minds. Except the poor, mad accountant, of course, who kept adding the same column of figures again and again. Again, the lover who keeps his love for a woman a secret in his own heart, never to be expressed to anyone, does not think that his love is a thought in his mind. If he did, he'd pull himself together perhaps, and say, 'Snap out of it, it's just infatuation'. A religious believer, of course, may come to think that 'God' is a thought in his mind. He may say, 'Why shouldn't I enjoy myself? There's no one there to stop me or to punish me.' Here, we would not say that the person is wrong because there *is* someone there, but that he was far away from what is meant by the fear of God. A philosopher too might say, 'If God is not an additional consciousness to all human consciousness, isn't he just a thought in my mind?' I can imagine how a philosopher can get into that state of mind. Clearly, however, when I have spoken of belief in God I have not been saying that God is a thought in my mind or anyone else's in any of these senses, so what Hick is trying to say or attribute to me remains unclear.

The main difference between Swinburne and Hick on the

one hand, and myself on the other, is that they think it is meaningful and necessary to discover a system or an order in human affairs. Belief in God, they would say, demands such an order. I do not think it makes sense to look for such an order and that belief in God is connected with a recognition of this fact.

My criticisms of Swinburne's treatment of moral realities do not depend on holding any particular moral point of view. Furthermore, if these moral realities had not been distorted, they would not have provided rational grounds either for or against religious belief. They would not be handmaids of a theodicy.

Hick says that the interest of a theodicy depends on 'its connection with an actual living tradition of religious faith, rather than being a mere *ad hoc* invention of philosophers'.[42] He says that 'the theodicy problem arises, for most of us at any rate,' as 'an inquiry concerning the rational possibility of an actual form of religious faith, such as the Christian faith'.[43] It is not clear whether the majority Hick refers to here is the majority of believers or the majority of philosophers of religion. He takes himself to be simply restating his point when he says, 'What we are asking is whether there are resources within that faith for meeting the problem of evil'.[44] I do not deny that when a believer in face of evil says, 'Lord, I believe, help thou mine unbelief' he is searching for such resources. What I deny is that those resources are the resources of a theodicy.

What responses can be made which are not responses in terms of a theodicy? Here, I offer only some suggestions, suggestions which I do not claim are all of a piece, capable of being fitted into a neat theological system. I have already suggested, in discussing what might be meant by someone who said the outcome was in the hands of God, that the force of the belief depends on the absence of the kind of higher level planning so essential to Swinburne's theodicy. The same is true of talk of God's grace in face of life's evils. In order even to reach the threshold of understanding what might be meant here, the sheer pointlessness of those evils has to be admitted.[45] One has to see, for example, that there is no reason why these natural disasters should not come our way. One has to be ready in face of one's cry, 'Why is this happening to me?' to reply 'Why shouldn't it?' This recognition of the pointlessness of suffering in this sense can lead in various directions. It has led some to speak of the absurd, but it has led others to speak of all things as God's gifts, and of things not being one's own by right or reason, but by the grace of God. It is not my purpose to advocate these uses of language, but simply to note their existence. Again, in other contexts, a person may wonder, in relation to his own character, what it is that he can do something about and what it is that has been given by God, that is that which cannot be changed but which he must come to terms with. On wider issues there may be much agonising over whether something, marriage, for example, is of God, something fixed and unalterable with which we must come to terms, or whether we are confusing a human institution with God's will and erecting a barrier with no more than a nominal reality which prevents us from receiving God's gifts of happiness.

Because these responses are not responses in terms of a theodicy, Hick talks of my disposing of the challenge of the problem of evil as though I did not allow for its reality. This is a good example of a philosopher thinking that if one does not agree with his conception of the bearing of religious belief on the evil in the world, one cannot believe that religious belief has any bearing on such issues. This is because the philosopher assumes that his conception of the connection between religious belief and suffering is the only possible one. It is this claim to have discovered 'necessities' and 'essences' that I am opposing. I am not ignoring the challenge of evil to religious belief, since in meeting a challenge the believer recognises its reality, otherwise there would be no need to meet it. His faith is tried and it may be defeated. The responses I have mentioned here and discussed elsewhere do not imply the dismissal of those considerations which have led people to talk of the problem of evil. On the contrary, without the human cry from the midst of afflictions no sense can be made of these religious responses, and there may be constant tensions of various kinds between the responses and the evils which surround them. The responses are not, however, recognitions of a higher order, but one way of understanding the lack of such an order. Even when the response is understood in this way, it may well be regarded by those who cannot share it as an evil response.

Hardy complains ironically in face of the limits and limitations Tess had to face or fail to face, that 'why so often the coarse appropriates the finer . . . the wrong man the woman, the wrong woman the man, many thousand years of analytical philosophy have failed to explain to our sense of order'.[46] In the context already mentioned I commented that Hardy, of course, was not looking for explanations. Swinburne and Hick look for explanations. Any sense of order with which one would have been satisfied would be defective just for that reason. That must be my verdict on Swinburne's theodicy. Swinburne admits that his God does ask a lot of his creatures, but says,

> A Theodicist is in a better position to defend a theodicy such as I have outlined if he is prepared also to make the further additional claim – that God knowing the worthwhileness of the conquest of evil and the perfecting of the universe by men, shared with them this task by subjecting himself as man to the evil in the world. A creator is more justified in creating or permitting evils to be overcome by his creatures if he is prepared to share with them the burden of the suffering and effort.[47]

Not so, for if the visit to our world were by such a God as Swinburne describes, those who said that there was no room at the inn would be right. We should not be at home to such callers. And if perchance we were asked to choose between this visitor and another, we should unhesitatingly demand, 'Give us Prometheus!'

Theodicies are part of the rationalism which I believe clouds our understanding of religious belief. I doubt whether any believer would deny that Jesus faced evil of a certain kind in the Garden of Gethsemane. And in asking that if possible the bitter cup should pass from him, he came to see his own survival as a mere possibility subject to the will of God. He came to see that the will of God meant, for him, the Cross. If anyone said that the Son of God met the evil in a reasonable way I would not know what to make of him. (Which is not to say that Jesus met the evil in an unreasonable way.) And if a philosopher attempts, as John Wisdom did once,[48] to show that the forgiveness from the Cross is reasonable, he gets into terrible trouble. I would at least venture to say that talk of reasonableness and rationality is not the most natural response of most Christians to the central act of their Faith.

Refusing to go down the road along which theodicies say we *must* travel is not to minimise the precariousness of religious faith or the trials and challenges it may have to face. It is simply to say that these are accounted for in terms other than those which theodicies offer us. As we have seen, Swinburne often distorts, in his analyses, religious and moral concepts which he believes others share. He believes this because he thinks that we must all think in a certain way about God and evil if we want to be rational about such matters. It is not enough, however, to point out his conceptual confusions, since if the ways of thinking expressed in this mode of philosophising become prestigious, they not only veil religious realities, but *replace* them with their own inventions. Our fate, in that event, is that this mode of philosophising presents its inventions as though they were the only ways of thinking which are available or ever have been available. The latter claim is false, but the claim about the present always threatens to be true. Ways of thinking may lose their hold on us, and philosophy may play a part in this. In the next chapter we turn to a consideration of the philosophical implications of this fact.

5 Belief, Change and Forms of Life

At the end of the last chapter I said that no serious account can be given of religious belief which does not take note of the way in which it is interwoven with the surrounding features of human life. It is how a religious belief is acted out in this context which determines what kind of sense, if any, it may have. That is why the importance of Wittgenstein's remark, 'To imagine a language is to imagine a form of life',[1] cannot be overestimated. Becoming acquainted with a language is not simply mastering a vocabulary and rules of grammar. It is to know how things bear on one another in such a way as to make it possible to say certain things and see certain connections, but not others. The same must be said for religion. It is a misunderstanding to speak of a religion *as* a form of life. What can be said is that it is impossible to imagine a religion without imagining it *in* a form of life.

What happens to a religion in a form of life cannot be laid down in advance. It is a matter of its fate in a complex network of influences and counter-influences. Among these influences, as we have seen, is the presence of philosophical activity of various kinds. This too contributes towards determining religion's fate. In this chapter we shall examine various relations in the form of life in which religion stands. We shall begin by examining how philosophy may itself threaten religion. This can be seen by examining the way in which Wittgenstein's insistence on the importance of the connection between language and a form of life has led to a polarising of views in the philosophy of religion in the last thirty years or so.

I EXTERNALISM AND INTERNALISM

If we look back to the 1950s, we find, in the literature, a certain kind of disagreement between philosophical believers and philosophical unbelievers which still persists today. The unbelievers suggested that the problematic core of religious beliefs was to be found, not in their falsity, but in their meaninglessness. The believers, on the other hand, argued that the beliefs were meaningful. By and large, however, the believers and the unbelievers agreed on the criteria of meaningfulness which had to be satisfied.[2] Under Wittgenstein's influence, some philosophers have suggested that these disputes are an irrelevance, since they never raise the question of whether the criteria of meaningfulness should have been agreed on in the first place. What has happened, it is suggested, is that criteria of meaning appropriate to certain aspects of human life and activity are made synonymous with meaning as such. One obvious example in our culture has been the tendency to elevate scientific criteria and procedures in such a way. What we ought to do by contrast, it was said, is to enquire into the meanings which religious beliefs have in the forms of life of which they are a part. Instead of constructing theories of meaning which determine what is to count as meaning, we should look at the use concepts actually have. This was the force of Wittgenstein's command, 'Don't think. Look!'[3] It constitutes an attack on what I shall call *externalism*.

As we have seen, following Wittgenstein's suggestions in the philosophy of religion seemed to bring problems of its own. What if we agree that various aspects of human life and activity, religion included, show forth distinctive meanings which must not be reduced to a spurious unity? Further, what if we also agree that philosophical confusions may be generated by the obscuring of these distinctive meanings? As we have seen in Chapters 1 and 2, to some philosophers it has looked as if the inevitable consequence is that we have divided human life into strict compartments, each autonomous as far as its meaning is concerned. We saw that five theses have been attributed to philosophers who are supposed to be prepared to embrace such consequences. Religious belief is said to be logically distinct from other kinds of belief. It may even be said that what is and is not meaningful in religion must be determined by criteria solely determined by the religion in question. It may then seem that religious belief cannot be criticised, can be understood only by participants, an absolute measure brought to bear on their lives. This measure, it is said, cannot itself be influenced, developed, changed or threatened by events in those lives, or by social or cultural events of any kind. It would follow from such views that religion would have been placed apart from history. This being so, how could anyone be worried about its future? Future, past or present could be no threat to it. Faith would be independent of temporal matters. The eternity which belonged to it would place it above such things. So far from trying to meet the criteria of meaning imposed on religious belief by externalism, this reaction simply declares that all external criteria of meaning are irrelevant to religious belief. Not unexpectedly, this reaction can be called *internalism*.

The price of internalism, however, is a high one. One might well apply to internalism remarks made by F. C. S. Schiller with respect to Kant's categorical imperative in ethics: '. . . it could not be convicted of failure to work, because it could never be required to work at all. Nay, it could glory in its uselessness, and conceive it as the proof of its immaculate purity'.[4] Religious beliefs begin to look like formal games, internally consistent, but unconnected with the day to day lives of men and women.

Like so many diametrically opposed theories in philosophy, internalism and externalism are thought to be the only alternatives. In fact, each alternative feeds off the deficiencies of the other. For example, because certain philosophers, including myself, attacked forms of externalism in the philosophy of religion, their critics assumed that they must hold the view I have called internalism. In the first two chapters I hope to have shown how mistaken this assumption is. As I said then, internalism is a philosophical invention which has attracted a certain amount of attention in the philosophy of religion because it was *attributed* to certain philosophers and *not* because it was a view held by those philosophers. Perhaps it could be argued that if we want to find something which approaches internalism we should look to theology rather than to the philosophy of religion. The early Barth seemed to get close at times to saying that if something was said with Biblical authority it did not have to answer *any* charge of incoherence. Interestingly, Barth was reacting against the kind of externalism found in certain forms of liberalism where what was distinctively Christian seemed to be sacrificed to the prevailing intellectual theories of the day. It was to this reductionism that Barth, rightly, said 'No!'

Advocates of externalism, in their turn, embrace their position because they think it necessary if the dangers of internalism are to be avoided. I had posed the problem as follows: 'Many religious apologists feel that if religious beliefs are not to appear as esoteric games they must be shown to be important . . . . What remains problematic is the way in which the apologists think the importance of religion can be established.'[5] I went on to criticise two influential externalist attempts to achieve this. First, an attempt to show that religious faith is more valuable than any other alternative, using 'value' as a relative term presupposing a common evaluative yardstick. Second, an attempt to show that religious belief is rational, by employing a notion of rationality which transcends belief and non-belief. I cannot repeat my criticisms here.[6] The previous chapter of this book, however, gave plenty of evidence of both externalist tendencies at work. Because I denied such external connections, critics, as we have seen, assumed that I denied connections of *any* kind between religious belief and other aspects of human life. If a man cannot support externalism, he must support internalism!

The connections between religious beliefs and what lies

around them are of a mixed character. Some of the connections which are called religious may be superstitious, while others cannot be characterised in that way. This illustrates well how internalism and externalism feed off each other's deficiencies. The externalist, seeing those religious beliefs which fall under wider criteria of intelligibility and yet infringe them, wishes to stress the accountability of religion in this respect. The internalist is accused of saying that anything called religion can determine what is meaningful in this context. The internalist, on the other hand, sees the distinctive character of certain religious beliefs, and does not want them to be misrepresented by the externalist's alien criteria of meaningfulness. Again, what is essential to realise is that we are not faced with a choice between these two positions. In emphasising that various aspects of human activity have distinctive criteria of meaning, it is easy, but mistaken, to deny that these various aspects are related to each other. Indeed, as we saw in the first two chapters, were it not for such relations the particular aspects could not have the distinctive meanings they do. For example, it may be confused to think that the harvest dance can be accounted for in the way one can account for the technology of the harvest. Some have thought that there was a causal connection between the dance and the harvest. In the last century writers suggested that the magical dance was a kind of primitive science. With the advent of modern technology, the day of the dance is over. The primitive assumption of a causal connection between the dance and the harvest is shown to be superstitious. We cannot argue *a priori* that this cannot be the case. Neither can we argue *a priori* that other possibilities of meaning do not present themselves. It is possible that superstition is to be found, not in the dance, but in those who want to explain it away. The dance can be seen as a celebratory activity. Wittgenstein reminds us in his 'Remarks on Frazer's *The Golden Bough*' that the dance for rain occurred when rain was due.[7] There is no causal connection between the dance and the coming of the rain. If there was thought to be such a connection, would people not dance in the long months of dryness and drought? The dancers do not cause the rain to come; they greet its coming. Dancing for rain is like dancing for happiness. Thus we can mark a conceptual difference between the dance and causal technology. Having seen the difference, however, it does not follow that the dance is unrelated to its surroundings. After all, what could a harvest dance be unless there were a harvest? Rituals could not constitute the whole of human life. Therefore, if there is a relation between the harvest dance and the harvest, what happens to the harvest may affect what happens to the dance. So although no account of the dance can be given in terms of technological causality, such technology may still affect the dance. If the values of technology become dominant and all-pervasive, the dance will come to be regarded as a waste of time.

What we have seen is that whether the meanings of religious practices are distinctive or not, one cannot ignore the relation between such practices and the human life which surrounds them. That being so, certain religiously comforting pictures have to be abandoned. It is appropriate to consider the first of these at this stage in the chapter. I shall consider others later. One might call the first comforting picture that of religious *individualism*. It appears to be something like this:

Christianity does not belong to the world of time. It is part of the eternal. The eternal cannot be dependent on the temporal. Therefore, whatever happens in the secular world which surrounds it, Christianity is eternally safe. There is a direct relationship between the believer and his personal Saviour. The believer who is saved has certainty in his heart. Whatever happens about him, the heart, the secret place, is safe from such influences. He does not have to worry about what happens to personal relationships, the family, the society or the culture, since the communion between the heart and the Saviour is direct, beyond the influence of personal, family, social or cultural events. Is not Heaven beyond the earth, and does not God in his Heaven see to it that the faith of the faithful is not frustrated? Therefore the nature of faith is beyond historical or cultural influences, since that faith is made secure by a transcendent cause, by no less than divine causality itself.

That is the comforting picture of religious individualism. But, as I have said, it is a picture which must be put aside. There is no necessity about the continued existence of Christianity. There is nothing in the nature of the universe, as it were, which guarantees this. There was a time before the existence of anything called a Christian culture, and there could be a time when it has disappeared from the face of the earth. It is this possibility that the comforting picture of religious individualism will not allow. According to the comforting picture, Christianity is safe in the believer's heart. The meaning is internal, beyond the reach of social or cultural influences. But does this make sense? What if someone suggested that Sarah, Abraham's wife, longed for the liberation of women in the sense in which this is widely sought in America today? The answer, of course, is that it is meaningless to attribute such longing to Sarah. It is meaningless because such ideas were not part of her world. But what if someone wanted to argue that the longing was something independent of all this, something internal in Sarah's heart? Would not the answer be that the possibility of a secret thought, even in the depths of the heart, depends on the limits of intelligibility within the culture. The limits of intelligibility determine possibilities of speech and thought. This is as true of secret thoughts as of public utterances. So you could not have a longing to be king in a culture where the notion of kingship has no meaning, and no knowledge exists of what it is to be a king in another culture. In the same way, Sarah cannot long for that which has no meaning for Sarah. This is not to argue against new developments or radical changes. Such developments and changes cannot be understood *in vacuo*, but must be seen against the background or in the context of the events in relation to which they occur. For these reasons, we cannot argue that Christianity has a hiding place in man's heart, since if the culture declines, in time there will also be a decline in the thoughts of men's hearts.

II RELIGIOUS BELIEF AND CULTURAL CHANGE

For all these reasons, the comforting picture of religious individualism has little substance. The Word cannot dwell among men no matter what the state of culture in which they live. Awareness of this fact has led many to ask today, 'What are we to do about the future of religion?' meaning, it seems, 'How can we make sure that religion has a future?' It seems to many philosophers that these questions can only be answered if one can show that religious belief is more worthwhile or more rational than any alternative in terms of some common measure of worthwhileness or rationality. In the absence of a common measure, how can there be *alternatives* to religious belief? How can belief be threatened, lost or replaced, if one denies the availability of such a measure? There is no simple answer to this question, but a number of possibilities which may arise serve to clarify the issue.

As we have seen, I have already denied that a firm religious belief means a belief firmly grounded according to the common measures mentioned. Because of such a denial, J. R. Jones asked me the following question: '. . . when belief is . . . undermined, or weakened, it then looks as though the picture itself begins to lose its hold on the life of the believer. And I wonder what this really signifies?'[8] The answers I gave to this question are, I believe, important in the context of our present problem. They can be divided into four kinds of response. First, I drew attention to the ways in which rival secular pictures constitute threatening alternatives to religious faith. Second, I indicated some of the ways religious faith may be characterised in face of such threats. Third, I spoke of cultural changes which may erode religious belief. Fourth, I asked what could be said if these changes were so pervasive as to destroy religious belief. It would be useful to elaborate on these four responses in order to appreciate the different contexts in which questions about the future of religion may arise.

First, then, I spoke of rival secular alternatives to religious faith. I had in mind here, principally, what religious believers would call temptations. These are present in any age in so far as most religions have called men away from certain activities and attitudes which are called sinful, unholy or unclean.[9] The philosophical difficulties for some philosophers have been to see how these can be assessed by a common measure. And, yet, should there be any difficulty? Consider the following example. There is a gentleman who appears advertising cigars on television. No sooner does this immaculate man light up cigars than women come from all quarters to gather round him. We can imagine people reacting in certain moods by saying, 'What a man!' Here, 'man' is clearly not a purely descriptive term. They are extolling, praising, wondering. A cluster of images influences their attitude: success, flair, charm, panache, the great seducer, etc., etc. At the heart of Christianity is a very different event. It is that of a torn body on a cross. Here, too, it was said, 'Behold, the man!' Do we need anything other than these two images to explain why they should be at war in the human soul? Once we elaborate their content we see how they cannot co-exist in peace within the same person. We do not need anything apart from these two visions, one of self-aggrandisement and the other of self-abnegation, to see why they generate conflict. The Christian will speak of the temptations of the flesh, while the pagan may complain of 'priests in black gowns walking their rounds and binding with briars' his 'joys and desires'. But from whichever direction the threat is thought to come, that one threatens the other cannot be denied. It seems as if we only have to expound the case for the conflict to become obvious.

Yet should we say that the conflict is obvious? There is no harm in this as long as one remembers that there are certain conditions within which it appears obvious. In other words, that the conflict appears obvious at a certain time does not mean that this reaction cannot be changed or eroded. I said that as soon as we expound the rival conceptions the tension between them becomes apparent, but it must not be forgotten that in expounding them thus two conditions are implied:

(a) that the state of society or culture is such as to enable such an exposition to be made;
(b) that the exposition does not fall on completely barren ground. The exposition, even if not heeded, is at least recognised.

Given these conditions, it is fairly easy to see how a religion may speak to the culture which surrounds it. The prophets of the Old Testament provide abundant examples of what I have in mind. They say, 'Thus saith the Lord . . .' and then proceed to rebuke people or nations for their evil ways. They call the wanderer back to a straight and narrow path. What is said from a religious point of view here at least has the possibility of being heard. It points out that covenants are being broken or disregarded, the tradition misrepresented, or points to possibilities of creative extensions of the tradition to meet new situations.

Second, in the face of threatening secular alternatives, religious beliefs may change their character. From the beginning, Christianity develops an *apologia* to meet the challenges which come from varieties of unbelief. A certain aspect of a culture, for example its science, may enjoy such prestige that the religious apologist may feel that he ought to be able to give an account of religion in the same terms. Matters become complicated when a particular *apologia* becomes a substantive part of faith for the believers. If such an *apologia* is not necessary to the faith, the faith becomes a mixture of the meaningful and the meaningless. The spiritual may become superstitious. For example, if what is important is conceived in terms of the ability to control, it may be difficult to think of other conceptions of importance. Religious belief may be advocated in the same terms. Religion, it is said, will give one the most extensive control of all over one's life. Indeed, it gives one control over what happens to one after death. It provides eternal security as distinct from temporal security.

Dominant conceptions of control may make it difficult, if not impossible, to see religious reactions for what they are. We have already seen the way in which some writers thought that the harvest dance was causally related to the harvest. They were blind to the celebratory character of the dance. Ironically, if the confused account enjoys sufficient prestige, the adherents of the dance may also come to think that unless the dance is causally efficacious it has no point. Confused reactions by believers to external threats may, in this way, distort and even erode the character of religious belief.

At this point we need to consider the third context, in which cultural changes may affect the character of religious responses to human life. I have in mind changes which cannot be said to be the fault of any single individual. Let us consider some examples. First, consider the effect of the development of birth control on the notion of life as a gift from God. How is it possible for believers to regard the birth of a child as a gift from God, while at the same time they urge their children to take advantage of contraception? How is it possible for believers to thank God for the birth of their child if they have been trying to plan it to the day, if possible, to take advantage of tax benefits? Perhaps it *is* possible, but at least there is a tension, a question to be resolved, since the notion of planning and that of a gift seem to be in conflict here. There is a danger of the religious words, even if they are used, seeming empty in the mouths of the believers. Again, religious responses may be eroded in seemingly more innocuous ways than this. It might be thought that traffic congestion has little to do with conceptions of death, apart from death on the road. Yet this is not so. Think of the ways in which the dead were accompanied to their graves. People walked with them to the end. They shared a last journey with them. Despite carriages, no one except the infirm thought of doing anything but walking. Then came the car. At first all seemed well. Even if people no longer walked, it was a solemn procession, one which pursued its way slowly and which no other traffic would cut across. As the car became economically within the reach of more people, wider roads were needed. Traffic congestion and the laws it generated became a problem for the solemn procession of the dead. The procession went faster, and the increased speed eroded the solemnity. Car-drivers no longer thought it necessary not to break the funereal procession. Slowly, but surely, factors which at first seemed to have little to do with religion eroded a religious response. With the coming of cremation, the mourners knew that they were not really there at the end anyway. Whereas earth was thrown on the coffin in their presence, everyone knew that the bodies were not cremated during the cremation service. How soon before it will be asked why, since we are not there at the end, should we take the body anywhere? Why not have it collected and taken to a central store from which it could be dispatched economically and hygienically?

Consider a final example in this context. Could hills declare the glory of God once gold has been discovered in them? Well, they might. The gold may be regarded as untouchable no matter how great the needs of the people. But if the hills are mined could the hills declare the glory of God? Again, they might. If the hills are only mined in face of real need, the hills might come to be regarded as the Great Providers. But what if the hills are mined because of the greed for gold? It is hard in these circumstances to see how the very same hills could declare the glory of God, since the act of exploitation, the utilitarian attitude to the hills, would jar with regarding the hills as belonging to God.

These examples may bring us to see why a second religiously comforting picture has to be put aside. The picture I have in mind may be called that of *religious rationalism*. It appears to be something like this:

No matter what cultural changes may take place, the validity of religious belief is secured by formal arguments which transcend the relativity of cultural contexts; arguments such as the ontological argument, the cosmological argument and the argument from design, all of which prove the existence of God. Reason is one, and transcends the kinds of considerations appealed to in this essay. Such considerations cannot affect the truths of reason where the existence of God is concerned.

As a matter of fact, I believe the exact opposite of this conclusion to be the case. So far from it being the formal proofs which give a rational foundation to the beliefs of the faithful, it was the lives of the faithful which breathed into the formal proofs whatever life they had. At a time when nature could be looked at as God's creation, when the heavens declared his glory, it is not hard to see how the intellectual expression of this religious response could take the form of an argument from design. The argument will not do. It is a poor shadow of what it is trying to express, but that it is trying to express it is the sole justification for its existence. Norman Kemp Smith suggests that this is why Hume and Kant, despite having exposed the formal inadequacies of the argument, kept thinking it worthy of the greatest respect when they turned to look at nature itself.[10] Similarly, at a time when the whole world could be seen as God's creation, it is not surprising that the attempt to express this intellectually could take the form of the cosmological argument. Faced with the formal inadequacies of the proof, some Neo-Thomists suggested that one could only understand the inference from world to God if one stood within, or took for granted, the cosmological relation.[11] Understood formally, this introduced a vicious circularity into the argument, since the cosmological relation is one of the things the argument is meant to establish. Nevertheless, the insight contained in the Neo-Thomistic suggestion lies in the appreciation of the religious response as logically prior to the attempt at intellectual elucidation. In his discussion of the ontological argument, Norman Malcolm has suggested that philosophers have thought the expression 'necessary existence' meaningless because they have ignored the human phenomena which give rise to the expression.[12] O. K. Bouwsma finds the argument to be 'the language of praise cooled down for purposes of proof' and finds the home of the derived expression 'that than which none greater can be conceived' in the language of praise in the Psalms and elsewhere.[13]

From these considerations, one can see how the comforting picture of religious rationalism must be put aside. If the argument from design, the cosmological argument and the ontological argument are attempts to give intellectual expression to the way nature may tell of God, the way the world can be seen as God's creation, the way God can be thought of as eternal, respectively, the arguments could not survive the demise of these religious reactions. Without the religious responses, the intellectual arguments would be no more than empty shells.

With the decline of these religious responses, we face a situation rather different from the first context in which we discussed mere deviations from the responses. There, as we saw, it made sense for the prophet's word to be a word of rebuke, a word of warning. In the present examples, we are discussing a context in which such rebukes would not mean anything. If a word of rebuke or warning is heard here, it is not a reminder of what they know already, but a new word for their critical time.

The fourth context concerning religion and culture is one in which not even a prophet or a lone visionary could be found. There would be no believers at such a time. Compare the absence of love in Aldous Huxley's *Brave New World*. Human relationships are spoken of in terms of sensation and transient need, much as if wine were being discussed. One might say to someone about to taste a second glass of wine, 'I wouldn't drink that if you've had some of that other kind. You need something different in between.' In Huxley's world one would say, 'If you've just had sexual relations with him or her, I wouldn't advise that one next, you need something different in between.' Of such a time one could say with J. L. Stocks that 'The convenience of a utensil would be the highest form of praise'.[14] Here, in terms of the language available, the possibility of love is ruled out. What could a word in the service of religion mean here? Clearly, there could not be a word *in* time in such a context. But might there be a word out of time, the beginning of a new possibility? This is a question to which I shall return later.

III RELIGIOUS BELIEF AND THE FUTURE

The examples I have considered, needless to say, are not meant to be any kind of historical or social survey, but are simply illustrations of the various relations between religious belief and conceptual change.[15] If we remember what we have said about the necessity for a connection between the Word of faith and various features of human life, and about the ways in which faith may be eroded, we can see that we are at the same time discussing religion's application to reality. Asking whether religion has any application to reality in the future is asking whether religion can speak to the future, whether it has anything to say. If religion has nothing to say, it has no future. True, its nominal existence may outlast its actual or authentic existence, but when that happens, religion is an edifice which, though standing, stands condemned. Many religious apologists are reluctant to countenance these possibilities. They take refuge in a third religious comforting picture, one I shall call, *religious accommodation*. It appears to be something like this:

So far, we have seen that there is a close connection between religion and culture. Without such a connection, religious beliefs would be formal practices of little significance. So there is no such thing as bare Christianity. From the beginning, Christianity responds to the culture surrounding it. Therefore, whatever the changes in our culture, however dark it becomes for certain religious traditions, Christianity can always accommodate the situation by taking on new cultural forms. If there is no such thing as bare, culture-less Christianity, Christianity can wear a new culture as it disposes of the previous one like an old garment. The question for Christianity in our day, therefore, is of how to come to a new cultural form which would contain an acceptable *apologia* to meet our contemporary crises.

What of this argument? It is a tempting thesis, but one which, I believe, like the two comforting religious pictures we have already considered, must be put aside if confusion is to be avoided. First, the relation between Christianity and culture is unlike the relation between a body and clothes. Although clothes may be changed, the identity of the body remains the same. But Christianity does not wear culture like a garment. Christianity is part of the culture; sometimes the most important part. Further, if we want to speak of a Christian tradition, there cannot be a complete break between the different periods in the history of the Faith. If we raise the question of God's identity, this has nothing to do with referring to an object. We did not learn the word 'God' in that way. We would determine whether two people are worshipping the same God by looking at the ideas which enter into their worship. So if we want to say that we worship the God of Abraham, Isaac and Jacob, there must be enough to link us with the past to enable us to claim that we are worshipping the same God. Yet, although this conceptual continuity is important, we cannot assume that this continuity can be guaranteed in any situation. This brings us back to the question of whether such continuity can be safeguarded in our time.

When believers see religious belief declining it is natural that they should long for some kind of reawakening. There is nothing misplaced in such a desire. What is misplaced is the thought that such an awakening could be made a matter of policy by the Church. If such a policy were possible, no doubt there could be discussions within the Church about the cultural forms which ought to be adopted in face of contemporary crises. But such discussions would harbour deep confusions.

What is the source of the confusion? Does it not consist partly in this: if there is a relation between religion and culture, and if the religious element expresses what is spiritual, it is important to realise that the religious element is a *contribution* to the culture and not simply a reflection of it. For example, Michelangelo's work does not reflect or illustrate religious ideas, but contributes towards such ideas. Similarly, Beethoven could not have given us the last movement of the Ninth Symphony unless there were conceptions of joy in human life. But Beethoven does not reflect those ideas; he contributes to them by extending them. To see how he does this we would have to speak about the last movement of the Ninth. What is deep in a culture did not come about as a matter of policy. Shakespeare, Beethoven and Tolstoy did not give us their work *in order* that we might have something excellent in culture. No, they gave us what they had to give and we found it was excellent. Perhaps the point can be clarified as follows: some time ago British universities were asked whether they wanted to be centres of excellence, as if that question made sense. Never had such unanimity been known in the academic senates of the land! Traditional enmities and oppositions were united as members indicated, solemnly, with raised hands, that they wanted to be a centre of excellence. A university, however, does not become a centre of excellence by trying to be one. On the contrary, we are fortunate if scholars give themselves to their subjects as best they can. The results may or may not be excellent.

Religious apologists have much to learn from these conceptual truths. The Church cannot speak to the culture in which it is placed by making this a matter of policy. No, it speaks and perhaps the consequences will be good. The Church cannot *decide* to speak with authority in the culture. It speaks and perhaps its voice will be authoritative. Jesus spoke as one having authority, not as one who decided to speak with authority. This is simply one instance of a wider truth. A movement, and a religious movement is no exception, flourishes when people are engaged in its particular concerns, not when they are preoccupied with its maintenance. One is characteristically concerned about maintenance, how to keep going, for example, in a marriage, when there is a threat of things falling apart. But, it may be said, things are falling apart, so why should not the Church be concerned with maintaining the faith? This form of words, in certain circumstances, may be unobjectionable. Even if they are not sufficient conditions for religious renewal, there are many social, political and cultural developments which the Church may recognise, with good reason, either to be or not to be in its interest. Yet the matter must be stated carefully. There is nothing in religion akin to carrying on for the sake of children in a marriage. What one must notice is that in the marriage example one settles for second best, but in the case of religion there is no second best once the spirit of faith has departed. One can have integrity in a marriage when love has died, but there is no such thing as integrity in religion when faith has gone.

The misconception comes from the way in which the religious apologist thinks a word in time may be found as a matter of policy in the time of crisis or in order to avert a crisis. Consider a parallel example.[16] After the horrors which the Jews suffered at the hands of the Nazis, many Jews have vowed that such a thing shall never happen again. Such a reaction is understandable. However, money was given to a university to conduct research into the reasons why the Nazis did what they did, and into the conditions for the rise of Nazism. The hope is clear. They thought that if such reasons and conditions could be determined, men could see to it that such atrocities did not occur again. There is confusion in this natural hope. What is needed in order to withstand such a possibility is a moral reaction and probably force of arms in the end. The moral reaction cannot be secured by a quasi-scientific enquiry. Similarly, if one were looking for the authoritative voice of the Church in our day, that voice would have to take a spiritual form; that is, and this is a matter of logic not of apologetics, the mode of the message must be as spiritual as its content. If an authoritative voice is heard it may be the voice of a new prophet, or perhaps something will be shown authoritatively through events which may befall the culture. The confusion is in the religiously comforting picture which suggests that any cultural shift can be accommodated by religious apologetics as a matter of policy.

IV OPTIMISM AND PESSIMISM

We have considered the relations between religion and culture in four different contexts. First, we saw how a word in time within a tradition is a word which is accepted as proclaiming, checking, warning, rebuking, etc. Second, religious apologetic may distort religious belief in its attempt to meet threatening secular alternatives to religious belief. The word may be ill served by its own adherents in this way. These alternatives may erode religious belief. Third, a tradition may be extended creatively to meet a crisis. Think of the way in which a word in time was needed during the Babylonian Exile. The people asked how they could sing the Lord's song in a strange land. Their difficulty was not lack of enthusiasm, but bewilderment. How could a god whose efficacy ended at the boundary sustain them in a strange land? There had to be an extension in the notion of the divine before the question could be answered. Yet here, the language of faith, creatively extended, becomes a word in time for the people. Fourth, we considered cultural contexts such as those depicted in Huxley's *Brave New World*, and raised the question of how faith could speak in it, what a word in time would mean here. From what we have seen so far, it should be clear that philosophy cannot argue for an *a priori* religious optimism or an *a priori* religious pessimism in face of these facts. Nevertheless, some philosophical insights can be gained by reflecting on why philosophy cannot argue in this way. To do this, we shall look again at the problem of evil which we discussed in the previous chapter.

We saw how evils of various kinds do pose real problems for religious belief. What, for example, does it mean to speak of a God of love in face of such evils? We saw too how the answers found in apologetics often take the form of tired theodicies which try to justify evil in terms of some greater good.[17] By contrast I hinted at the notion of grace found in the reflections of Simone Weil; a notion which has, as a precondition, the recognition of the pointlessness of evil. In secular thinkers we have seen reactions of protest, rebellion, or absurdity. The sheer given character of unavoidable evil, for Simone Weil, shows, because of the very absence of reasons and explanations, that nothing is ours by right in this context. There is a precariousness about human life which can give birth to a view of life as a gift – a gift from God. My aim in recalling these remarks from the last chapter is not to elaborate them further, but to show how difficulties can arise, not only for Swinburne's theodicy, but at *this* level too.

Allowing, then, for Simone Weil's view, which, I realise, for many, would be to allow too much, God being with man in his suffering has to do with the realisation of grace in face of the pointlessness of evil. The ability to accept all things from God is part of what she means by love of the beauty of the world. It also necessitates fighting against those relations and conditions which she believes militates against the possibility of this beauty being revealed. It is in contexts such as these that she speaks of Christianity offering a use for suffering, but no remedy for it. Although Jesus calls out on the Cross, 'My God, my God, why hast thou forsaken me?' experiencing the void, the pointlessness, he was able to commit himself into his Father's hands.[18]

But does evil always allow for such reactions? Simone Weil acknowledges that there can be afflictions of such extremity that even the possibility of a cry is ruled out. The human becomes a vegetable. How does the death of Jesus speak to this case, since, as I have said, Jesus was not deprived of the ability to cry out? Consider examples from the two extremes of the human spectrum. What of the baby thrown up and caught on the bayonet? What of the incomprehension of the senile? In the case of the child, conditions have not yet developed in which what Simone Weil would call 'being with God' can be realised. With the senile these conditions have deteriorated beyond recall. I am not saying that the words 'Yea though I walk through the valley of the shadow of death I will fear no evil for thou art with me' *could not* mean anything in these circumstances, but it is difficult to see what they *do* mean. It is one thing to see one's own sufferings in relation to God's will, and quite another to see other people's sufferings in that way. Clearly, if we are to say that God is in the sufferings of others, especially in the extreme cases I have indicated, this cannot mean that the sufferer is aware of God's presence. Here, it may be said, there is an important distinction between what can be *said* in suffering and what can be *shown*. This is not an easy distinction to uphold in all circumstances. There are cases where a believer, in making a sacrifice, knows in making it that it may destroy him; perhaps even that it will involve him in regretting making it. Here, his foreknowledge may make it possible to see his sacrifice as of God, even where he has been deprived of the ability to worship. In the examples of the child and the senile, however, it makes no sense to speak of a conviction of any kind being present. Others may say that this very senselessness shows that such examples do not count against the intelligibility of religious faith. To think otherwise is to think that God's omnipotence is the ability to do the impossible. God's power is the power of love. God's activity therefore is the activity of divine love, something which it would not make sense to think of as present in a person unmediated by his personality. To say that God is with all men, on this view, is to say that in all cases, where it makes sense to say so, the possibility of coming to a recognition of divine grace is open to all men. But what does this possibility amount to? Is it not possible, as many writers discussed in the previous chapter pointed out, for suffering and evil to lead to very different reactions? Suffering may lead to meanness and pettiness. My aim in mentioning these issues is not to resolve them, but to illustrate the kind of considerations which may arise when people grapple with these issues. It is an area where, for the philosopher, dogmatism is singularly out of place. Consider the following example which is impressively ambiguous.

In one of his early works, *Night*, Elie Wiesel tells of the deportation of Elisha and his young family from their village in Eastern Europe to Auschwitz and Buchenwald. In these horrific circumstances Jews had to face a crisis of faith. What could it mean now to speak of themselves as God's chosen people? Wiesel writes of three hangings at Auschwitz, one of them involving a child:

> The SS seemed more preoccupied, more disturbed than usual. To hang a young boy in front of thousands of spectators was no light matter. The head of the camp read the verdict. All eyes were on the child. He was lividly pale, almost calm, biting his lips. The gallows threw its shadow over him.
>
> This time the Lagerkapo refused to act as executioner. Three SS replaced him.
>
> The three victims mounted onto the chairs.
>
> The three necks were placed at the same moment within the nooses.
>
> 'Long live liberty!' cried the two adults.
>
> But the child was silent.
>
> 'Where is God? Where is he?' someone behind me asked.
>
> At a sign from the head of the camp, the three chairs tipped over.
>
> Total silence throughout the camp. On the horizon the sun was setting.
>
> 'Bare your heads!' yelled the head of the camp. His voice was raucous. We were weeping.
>
> 'Cover your heads!'
>
> Then the march past began. The two adults were no longer alive. Their tongues being swollen, blue-tinged. But

> the third rope was still moving; being so light, the child was still alive . . .
>
> For more than half an hour he stayed there, struggling between life and death, dying in slow agony under our eyes. And we had to look him full in the face. He was still alive when I passed in front of him. His tongue was still red, his eyes were not yet glazed. Behind me, I heard the same man asking: 'Where is God now?'
>
> And I heard a voice within me answer him: 'Where is He? Here He is – He is hanging here on this gallows . . .'
>
> That night the soup tasted of corpses.[19]

I realise that most expositors of Wiesel's work have not seen any ambiguity in this reaction to the death of the child. They have said that for Wiesel, the death of the child shows the death – the irrelevance – of God. It certainly implies the death of a religion of compensation, a religion which promises to see that things turn out all right. But does it deny the possibility of any kind of religious response? I am not sure. Wiesel is writing of the Jewish Faith, and it would be presumptuous of me to say what is or what is not possible in this context. In Christianity, however, is there not a further possibility, the possibility of 'He is hanging here' meaning, not, the demise of the divine, but its identification? The servant at the heart of Christianity is, after all, a suffering servant, a religious notion known, of course, in the Jewish Faith also.

It is not for me, even if I could, to attempt to spell out in detail what these religious reactions amount to. This is no accident. If words or events can speak of God even in face of the sufferings of others, those words or events will have the authority which comes of spirituality. To think that philosophical analysis as such could be the source of such authority would be to have misunderstood the whole import of this chapter. If a philosopher were to entertain such hopes as a philosopher it would be a comic presumptuousness on his part. Yet it must be said that this presumptuousness is often found in theological and philosophical apologetics. As I have said, the construction of tired theodicies is a case in point.

Many would say that the language of faith shows this tiredness more generally in our culture. No statement on a large scale seems possible. It has been said that the search for a religious syntax in the New English Bible has led to a loss of authority in that language.[20] There can be no *a priori* optimism about our ability to restore this deficiency. This is partly what Beckett shows us in *Krapp's Last Tape*. Beckett's character tries to make a new tape:

> Now the day is over,
> Night is drawing nigh -igh,
> Shadows – (coughing, then almost inaudible)
> of the evening
> Steal across the sky.[21]

He fails. He throws the new tape away and puts an old tape on once more in an attempt to recapture a moment of passion which happened long ago. But there is no comfort to be found there either:

> Here I end this reel. Box – (pause) – three, spool – (pause) – five. (Pause). Perhaps my best years are gone. When there was a chance of happiness. But I wouldn't want them back. Not with the fire in me now. No, I wouldn't want them back.[22]

Krapp is 'motionless staring before him. The tape runs on in silence'.[23]

There is nothing new to say. It is too late to bring the past back. That is one lesson, at least, that Beckett's character has learnt – 'But I wouldn't want them back . . . . No, I wouldn't want them back'. The present a failure, and the past gone. 'The tape runs on in silence'. This is a difficult lesson for religious apologists to accept. Yet it would be difficult to deny that religion faces dark times, at least in the English-speaking world. The language offered is tired and inadequate. Efforts on a wider scale fail.

Yet it must be remembered that if *a priori* optimism cannot be justified, neither can *a priori* pessimism. It is tempting to conclude that if such a time as Huxley's *Brave New World* came about, religious faith would be impossible, since the conditions from which it could sustain itself are lacking. This reaction is mistaken. For any religious reaction we may care to think of, we can imagine cultural changes which would deprive it of the surroundings in which it flourishes. Yet the philosopher has no right to infer from this that religious responses will not take new forms. What we have seen is that these cannot be made a matter of policy. The new forms do not arise because we decide that they shall arise. When Beethoven's music arrived it was possible to see connections between it and the tradition he inherited. Yet his coming could not have been predicted on the basis of such a tradition. Similarly, if a new prophet were to come, we would see a host of connections between his words and the state of our society and culture. But, again, this does not mean that we can foresee his coming on the basis of our present situation.

On the other hand, there can be no necessity about such an awakening. Perhaps in the future the tape is to run on without any mention of Christianity. If this came to pass, the situation would be at a further extreme from that depicted by Beckett, since no one would know that there had been anything religious on the tape in the first place.

Many apologists find these conclusions disturbing. In the final chapter of the book we begin by asking why this should be so. Some of the misgivings, as we shall see, are the products, at least partly, of philosophical confusions. Further, such misgivings can lead to a characteristic annoyance with the philosopher. If the philosopher is so anxious to explore the philosophical implications of religion's cultural predicaments, why cannot philosophy *itself* offer solutions for such predicaments? Why can we not look forward to the emergence of a Christian philosophy?

6 Can There Be a Christian Philosophy?

The relationships between philosophy and theology are complex and in the present chapter my intention is not to give anything like a historical survey of what these have been or what they are now. Such a survey would simply relate the facts, pointing out wide and marginal differences in the very notions of philosophy and theology, and, consequently, in the conceptions of the relation in which they stand to each other. Here, the issue of the relation between philosophy and theology is itself a problem posed by the course our argument has taken. That argument itself creates philosophical questions which need to be answered. In the light of the course which the philosophical analysis has taken, we find that some theological responses become problematic. For example, in the previous chapter, we saw how, given a readiness to countenance certain forms of cultural change, three comforting religious pictures, religious individualism, religious rationalism, and religious accommodation have to be abandoned. But what if the theological response refuses to countenance the cultural changes we mentioned? Is philosophy's critical reaction to such a confusion a matter of trespassing on a domain where it has no business to be? Is the theological refusal itself a product of conceptual confusion and therefore a proper object of philsophical concern? This is one way in which the issue concerning the relation between philosophy and theology arises naturally from the course our enquiry has taken. Let us now explore it further.

In Chapter 2 we were reminded of one of the reasons why Wittgenstein introduced the term 'language-games' into his philosophy. He wanted to emphasise, over and over again, that distinctions between sense and nonsense do not exist in abstraction, in an *a priori* realm prior to all experience. We master the distinctions between sense and nonsense, we see what these come to, only in the contexts of the language-games we play and the way they bear on one another. When we look at those phenomena, we can say, 'Human life is like that'. But something in theologians and philosophers of religion may want to say more, to say, 'Human life *must* be like that'. The difficulty is to see the warrant for this 'must'. On what could this dogmatism be based?

We must remind ourselves again that 'new language-games . . . come into existence, and others become obsolete and get forgotten'.[1] Could those language-games that mean most to religious believers be among those that become obsolete and get forgotten? People differ about this. Some will say that they can imagine it, while others will be unable to do so. So far, these are differences in prediction and, as such, are of no philosophical importance. The religious apologist may want to go further, to say that because of some kind of necessity – the necessary consequence of divine activity operating on the world from outside space and time, the necessary structure of language, the necessary character of the world, the necessary character of human nature – religious language-games *could not* pass away. We are not given a clear account of what this 'could not' amounts to. The apologists know well enough that the necessity of the continued existence of language-games cannot be hardened into logical necessity, and yet they want it to be more than a mere prediction. What exactly they want it to be cannot be said, since this is characteristic of the conceptual confusion they are in. This confusion may take different forms.

Apologists may think that there is some kind of contradiction involved in saying that the eternal truths of religion may pass away from the face of the earth. For obvious reasons, such a prospect is a terrible one for believers, but is it one that contradicts their faith? Some would think so. Has not the eternal become dependent on the temporal? Can one still speak of religious truths as eternal in face of those considerations?

The answer is that we can, because the considerations themselves harbour confusions. If what is required in order to make religious truths eternal, in the sense of non-precarious, is to make their continued existence in a culture secure, immune from all contingencies, we have already seen enough in the course of the book to realise why such a requirement cannot be granted. In such contexts, religious truths are as precarious as anything else. This does not mean that the beliefs are not absolute or eternal in the sense this has in religion. It is possible, given the grammar of such beliefs, to say something now about a time when no one believed in God. The believer can say that such a world has turned its back on God, or that God has judged such a world by ceasing to reveal himself in it. The absolute demands which belief makes on believers, the way the character of the beliefs as eternal truths expresses the turning away from worldliness to spirituality – none of this would be less true for a believer because the majority, or even all mankind, ceased to believe in such things. After all, that is not why the believers put their trust in these truths in the first place.

In the Fifth Book of *The Prelude* Wordsworth discusses his fear that the whole world of learning might be destroyed. Even if this were to happen, he believes that new awakenings of creativity would occur. What is of interest, however, is the effect on the status of the works even if they are destroyed. He longs for the existence of these works among men to be made permanent and wonders

> . . . why hath not the Mind
> Some element to stamp her image on
> In nature somewhat nearer to her own?
> Why, gifted with such powers to send abroad
> Her spirit, must it lodge in shrines so frail?

Similarly, believers may wonder why the truths of their faith are in earthen vessels. Yet Wordsworth does not confuse the issue of the extent of human allegiance to learning with the character of the learning he extols. When he considers poetry and geometry in this context, this is how he speaks of them:

> On poetry and geometric truth,
> And their high privilege of lasting life,
> From all internal injury exempt
> I mused;[2]

The lasting life which is exempt from all internal injury has clearly nothing to do with continued duration. It has to do with what geometry and poetry are capable of expressing. The 'eternity' found in these contexts is not the same as that which religions talk of. Nevertheless, in religion too it is important not to confuse 'lasting life', in the sense of surviving contingencies, with what is expressed by religious truths. It is in this latter context, if at all, that sense can be made of an eternity 'from all internal injury exempt'. To seek exemption from external injury too is to seek what cannot be obtained in the interests of a confused conception of eternity.

It may be thought, however, that there are reasons *within* a particular religion which lead one to deny that a time may come when no one believes in God, or when God no longer reveals himself in the world. This may be thought to be the case where Christianity is concerned. It may be said that all revelations before the birth of Jesus are partial, necessarily incomplete. Once the final and complete revelation has been received, however, it is no longer open to the believer to say that that revelation may not be present in the world, or that God will not continue so to reveal himself. It may be partly for this reason that so many theologians embrace what I called, in the last chapter, the comforting picture of religious accommodation. They believe that faith can always accommodate whatever changes occur in human life.

Even from a theological viewpoint, it could be argued that

the above conclusions need not follow. It is one thing to say that one believes that, as a matter of fact, God will not leave himself without a witness in the world, but quite another to say that should that come about, it would constitute some kind of contradiction within the Faith. A theologian could believe that a complete and final revelation had been given to the world, and still believe also that the degree of acceptance given to the revelation may vary considerably from age to age. The belief that a revelation is final need not entail the view that its acceptance is guaranteed. The acceptance it is given may wax and wane. To think that its acceptance is guaranteed seems to assume that the revelation has a guaranteed efficacy in the hearts of men. The offer of a truth, however, does not guarantee its acceptance. On the contrary, we are reminded that when the light came, the darkness comprehended it not.[3] In this respect, we can compare faith with great love poetry. It has been said that all great love poetry says the same thing. The task of the poet in every age comes from the fact that the same thing cannot be said in the same way. The same thing must be said, but it must be said differently in every age. From this, however, it cannot be assumed that 'saying it again, but differently' is always a possibility. There may be times when the poetic voice is in a minor key, genuine, but muted. At such a time, it is of the first importance that this is recognised. 'Saying it' can only be known via memory or acquaintance with examples from times other than one's own.

Such recollection can ensure that what is minor is not confused with the major, that the muted voice is not taken to be clarity. Cannot all this be true of the voice of faith too? If religion is in the valley rather than on the mountain-top, it is as well that this is recognised. A clear voice may be absent, clarity being seen only in recollection of times past. At such a time, as we have seen, patience is called for, in the realisation that the emergence of an authentic spiritual voice cannot be attained as the result of any kind of policy.[4] We have seen also how important it would be, at such a time especially, to put away the comforting religious pictures of religious individualism, religious rationalism and religious accommodation. Furthermore, it would be essential to exercise a kind of *via negativa*, the task of seeing to it that the spurious does not become a readily accepted substitute to fill the void created by the loss of religious authority. Of course, the matter is far more complicated, since the void may be due to the fact that the spurious has already been embraced. Contemporary theological disputes on such matters are therefore, of necessity, tortuously inconclusive, since one party is trying to tell another that it has embraced or been embraced by spurious conceptions of the faith. The very nature of this accusation, in the vast majority of cases, rules out the likelihood of the reply, 'Yes, that is precisely what we have done'!

So far, the discussion in this chapter has been of the background against which the question with which we ended the previous chapter emerges. When a philosopher stresses the possibility of religious language-games being forgotten or becoming obsolete, the multiplicity of social movements which may erode religious belief, the possibility of a faltering faith which never quite manages to tell the old, old story again, he may be asked, in return, what *he* has to say about it, what *he* takes the truth to be, how *he* would tell the old story again.[5] When such questions are asked there is a necessary tension between the response of the theologian and the response of the philosopher. If we could be clear about the character of this tension, we would also be clearer about why there cannot be a Christian philosophy.

I spoke earlier of the complex relationships between philosophy and theology, recognising that there are different conceptions of philosophy and theology. I realise that the relations I am about to explore exclude certain traditions of thought, and even certain conclusions within the same tradition. For example, I am not concerned with philosophy as reflection on the wisdom of the fathers. For present purposes, that would be a kind of secular 'theology'. Further, and more familiarly in the context of the present book, I am not going to rehearse again arguments concerning the meaningfulness of religious language. As we all know, for many philosophers that issue has been settled long ago: that language is meaningless. Obviously, there can be no Christian philosophy for them, unless all one means by this term is philosophical reflection on Christianity. The faith is weighed in the scales and found wanting. Such philosophers carry on disputes with others who deny their conclusions, but who weigh faith in more or less the same scales. They do not find the faith wanting. On the contrary, for them, it passes the test they have set it. No, let us agree with those who have said that philosophers on *both* sides of *that* dispute had better look again at what they are doing. It is not that they have weighed incorrectly, but that they have to discard their scales. They have assumed, too readily, that all forms of discourse have the same character. For present purposes let us assume what, unfortunately, is not the case, namely, that inspection has done the trick and that matters have been rectified. Wittgenstein's advice has been taken, 'Don't think. Look!' and, having looked, let us say, philosophers and theologians agree on the grammar of certain religious beliefs and activities. Would agreement even of such a specific kind obliterate the differences between philosophers and theologians? I think not.

The matter is complicated because theologians may avail themselves of philosophical resources. Let us consider an illuminating example of what I have in mind in the work of a theologian who wants to clarify the aim of theology.[6]

Charles Wood reflects on Luther's remark that 'Divinity is nothing but a grammar of the language of the Holy Ghost' and compares it with Wittgenstein's parenthetical remark, 'Theology as grammar'.[7] Wood stresses, quite rightly, that the language of scripture, like all other language, has its life in its use. Scripture is not 'the product of divine dictation, the Spirit's own words recorded by human amanuenses'.[8] On the contrary, it is a human language in which the Spirit speaks. I say *in* which it speaks, rather than *through* which it speaks, since this latter way of putting it may suggest a message which language struggles, but never quite manages, to convey.

Wittgenstein warned against the assumption that thought is to language what melody is to a song. He might have spoken in the same way of 'spirit' in the present context. Take away the lyrics of a song, and you still have the melody. Take away the language and what is the thought or the spirit of the word? Without the word there is no thought or spirit. All thought need not be in words and the spirit of a message may be in dance or gesture. Yet, for such activities to have a meaning, they must have a place among a people who speak a language. Without such a place it has no life. Wood says that the language of scripture may become the language of the Holy Spirit when 'it functions as such in the lives of its readers and hearers; when, perhaps, it grants them a new apprehension of the ultimate context of their lives, or new attitudes, or new concepts, or sustains and strengthens those previously granted – when it opens to them the life of faith, hope, and love, and nourishes them in that life.'[9]

Wood's emphasis here may give the impression of too individualistic a view of the relation of a person to the language of faith. Nothing of what he says need be lost if one stresses how a living language creates possibilities for a person for the first time when he makes its domain his own. Thus, if the scriptures come to a people in a great English translation, that translation may have been inspired precisely in the way Wood speaks of. Similarly, a translation may be uninspired and yet enjoy contemporary prestige for other reasons. Such a language, born in unfortunate surroundings, can only become alive in use in unfortunate ways. This is why the moment of translation is a momentous one for any holy writ, and why the assumption that the resources for translation are always available is such a dangerous one. With such reminders in mind, we can assent to Wood's conclusion that 'insofar as Christians understand themselves to be the historically formed covenant people of God, whose charter and text is that collection of documents known as the Old and New covenants, scripture will always be more than either a source of ideas or a canon of critical reflection, as it functions in numerous ways to nurture and shape the life and language of that people.'[10] But, Wood asks, 'what does it mean to speak of theology as the grammar of that language in which the Spirit speaks?'[11] It is in this context that he explores what is meant by theology as grammar.

First, he suggests, theology is a grammar in the sense that it tells us what can and cannot be said in various circumstances:

> Theology as grammar, then, tells us how to take the language of faith. It discloses its sense. It is an aid to those who would speak and understand that language, helping them to avoid mistakes and misapprehensions so that they can get along with the language. It is especially helpful, it may be supposed, where the requirements of faithful speaking put some strain on ordinary grammar, as in Luther's example, or where apparent similarities to other sorts of language may mislead the hearer, or where a new context or a new challenge calls for new developments in the language. Does the Christian doctrine of creation imply a hypothesis concerning the origin of the species? How may the concepts of sin and salvation be related to psychological understandings of the human condition and human potential? What is the bearing of Christian hope upon social and political struggle?[12]

We can see why, given such examples, Wood can say that 'People have recourse to theology as to a grammar, when they become aware of some difficulty in their understanding and use of the language, or when they want to gain proficiency of a certain sort'.[13]

Gaining proficiency, however, need not be connected with moments when the language has become difficult for someone. There is a use of 'theology' where it indicates the governing role of central beliefs in a religion. 'God is love', for example, is not a description of God, but is, in certain religions, a rule for the use of the word 'God'. 'God is not love' would not be a denial of an attribute which God happens to have, as John happens to be tall, but a denial of the reality of God. In Christianity, for example, we are told that it does not make sense to say that a man can love God while hating his fellow man. Theology as grammar, in this context, determines what can and cannot be said of God. It is present as soon as one has a religious language, however primitive. We cannot ask which came first, the theology or the language, any more than we can ask which came first in the case of logic and language.[14] Here, there is no parallel role for philosophy in relation to religion. Philosophy itself cannot lay down what sort of god people are to worship.

Yet, even in the context Wood emphasises, where theology does aid those who run into difficulties with religious concepts, there are important differences in the interest of the philosopher in the same context. Clearly, in Wood's examples, there are overlaps between philosophy and theology. Both the philosopher and the theologian may address themselves to the question of whether the doctrine of creation implies a hypothesis about the origin of the species. Yet, even though the question is the same, what commends it is different. The theologian is the servant of a faith and it is in order to enhance that faith that he wants to be clear about it. The clarity is a means to a further end. That is not so in philosophy. The clarity is an end in itself. The theologian is an aid 'to those who would speak and understand' the language of faith. The philosopher wants to be clear about the character of that language. He may not want to speak it. The theological enterprise has an aim. In relation to the faithful it helps them 'to avoid mistakes and misapprehensions so that they can get along with the language'. The philosopher's search for clarity is to see what kind of language is involved here, whether or not he, personally, can get along with it or not.

The same difference emerges in the second set of answers Wood provides in elucidating the role of theology as grammar. It may be thought that grammar is always backward-looking, stipulating what can and cannot be said in the light of what is already known. Even when difficulties arise, they may be thought of as difficulties concerning what is already established. Yet, as Wood has already half-suggested, this would ignore the role of grammar in creative extensions of a language. In the empiricist tradition, language was conceived of as the verbalisation of a given stock of ideas. Novelty, on this view, seemed to be little more than a reshuffling of the pack. Wittgenstein, on the other hand, stressed the open-ended character of conceptual rules. Conceptual rules may be extended, although one cannot determine *a priori* the range of such extensions. Wood shows how theology as grammar may bring about such extensions in the language of faith:

> It allows us to judge, with all due trepidation, the extent to which the language of our past and present may have furthered or hindered its own authentic aim. That is, it permits the criticism of tradition and of current practice. At the same time, a grasp of the grammar enables one to participate responsibly in the extension, reformulation, and general growth of the language of the community which seeks to bear witness to God.[15]

Again, the call to witness determines the nature of the task. The philosopher is not called to witness, but to clarify. The philosopher's call is not to follow the revelation, but to follow the argument. Of course, the tasks will overlap at many points. The philosopher may point out confusions which would make proposed extensions of the language of faith not extensions at all. Whether he is heeded is another matter. Yet, even if such confusions were fully explored and recognised, the philosopher, in all probability, will still be faced with a range of theological grammars. Wood speaks of *the* authentic aim of the language of faith, but I am sure he would agree that there is no general agreement about what this authenticity comes to. There is conflict between denominations and sects at various points. Here, it seems to me, theology is not an all-embracing arbitrator. On the contrary, the theologies understood as grammars are internally related to the different traditions, laying down what is of primary and secondary importance. Clearly, from what we have already seen, philosophy is not an arbitrator between different religious traditions. What, then, is the difference between philosophy and theology? A theological grammar seems to be the plotting of the co-ordinates of the tradition, marking as explicitly as possible what can and cannot be said. It may also endeavour to determine what the attitude of the tradition in which it operates ought to be with respect to different traditions. No serious believer can think that the question of which theology he embraces is a matter of indifference. It is too serious a matter for that. Philosophy will be interested in this phenomenon of co-operating and conflicting grammars. It will note the role of theology as grammar, and the kind of thing that counts as judgements of right and wrong in these contexts. For example, it will note that for the most part these judgements of authenticity and unauthenticity are not theoretical judgements. The philosopher concludes, 'In this neck of the woods, human life is like that'.

Wood is quite right in his emphasis on theology as the servant of the primary language of faith. He is aware of the dangerous consequences involved in theology wanting to be more than a grammar of the language of faith:

> A grammar is not a translation. It does not tell us in other words what the original language means. It is not a second language, superseding the primary idiom, but, simply, a guide to the use of that primary idiom. Theology has sometimes been understood as a new language, and theologians have occasionally tried to demonstrate the adequacy of their theological model by translating as much of the language of faith as they could into the new parlance.[16]

Wood says that what this amounts to is 'to produce a new vocabulary and conceptuality, a new home for Christian meaning'.[17] But, of course, the proponents of such an exercise will not be content with this characterisation. On this view, the theology in question is no more than the grammar of an alternative religious tradition. The proponents of the view, on the other hand, will want to entertain far larger dogmatic and essentialist claims. They will want to say that they have provided a conceptual grounding for the faith such that its rationality and the irrationality of its denial can be demonstrated. Here, an ambitious marriage is undertaken between philosophy and theology which must end in early divorce. On this view, Christian theology finds itself in the same category as Marxism and Freudianism as a form of *theoretical* dogmatism and essentialism. They offer, respectively, the economic, the sexual, as *the* key to everything, and the Christian theoretician will offer 'God'. All three say, 'Human life *must* be like that', and all three are wrong for similar reasons. All three will inevitably misdescribe the variety of phenomena in human life simply to bolster their respective categories. Such enterprises will lead to a condescending misunderstanding: it will involve saying in reality there is only one big fundamental game and that all the other games are partial aspects or distortions of it. Marx and Freud become involved in notorious difficulties by such efforts and a similar fate awaits the theologian who is not content with theology as a grammar of faith.

The denial of theology as the source of the rational foundation of *all* activities may be thought to restrict faith's sphere of influence in an undesirable way. This is not so. We smile at the harassed minister who responds to every book he hears commended by asking, 'Any sermons in it?' but he has a point. A serious theologian *will* need to relate all aspects of human life to the language of faith. But this is itself a theological and not a theoretical undertaking. It is one of the tasks of theology as grammar in extending the language of faith that Wood talks of. It is this which makes it distinct from such enterprises as Marxism and Freudianism. The theoretical implications of these enterprises involve redescribing the human phenomena by which they are confronted. They have to say, 'You think you are doing this, but *we* can tell you what you are really doing.' They then, suffering from a craving for generality, redescribe the phenomena in terms of their own dogmatic categories. Theologians, on the other hand, need not do this, even when they talk in terms of the dogmas of the faith. They can tell those who engage in perspectives very different from their own, 'We do not deny your description of what you are doing. It is exactly as you say. We do not want to *redescribe* it, but we do want to *judge* it in the light of the Christian revelation. What we do is not to show you the true rational foundation of what you have been doing all along. On the contrary, we offer you a new way, a way which may appear a scandal from your present point of view. What you need is not deeper reflection on what you are doing, but a change of direction.'

It may be asked by what authority this judgement is made. There is no answer outside the content of the revelation. When I say, 'this box is red' I am describing the colour of the box. When I say, pointing to a colour chart, 'this is red', I am not describing anything. I am teaching you what 'red' means. When Christians appeal to Christ, they are not applying to him a preconceived notion of truth. They are saying to us, 'This revelation is what we mean by "truth" '. Christ *is* the measure, not what is measured. The invitation, 'taste and see that He is good', is not an invitation to predicate preconceived notions of goodness to Christ, although these, as we have seen in previous chapters, have a part to play. In the main, it is to say, 'taste and see why this is what we now call "goodness" '.

The philosopher will be interested in seeing clearly what the theologian is doing here. But he will also be interested in seeing what others do in similar ways from within different perspectives. The philosopher is not the servant of any of them. Thus, even if religion were to pass away, philosophy, unlike theology, would not pass away with it. I am not saying that no conditions could arise which would be inimical to the pursuit of philosophy, but the disappearance of religion is not one of them.

We can see now why there is a necessary tension between philosopher and theologian if someone asks, when religion faces crises, 'What are you going to do about it? What is your answer to the situation?' If the questions were connected with puzzles concerning how one perspective can be used to judge another if it cannot call the other perspectives irrational and present itself as the true rational explanation of them, the philosopher, as I hope I have shown, certainly has something to say. But the questions sought more than that. They asked the philosopher to plot the connections which one perspective, in this case a Christian one, *ought* to make between itself and others. This cannot be a philosophical enterprise. It is theology, not philosophy, which has the task of evolving a grammar for such connections. The philosopher's comments on perspectives do not constitute in themselves an *additional* perspective. His comments serve to clarify conceptual confusions. In illustration of this consider the comments with which Norman Malcolm ends the preface to his *Problems of Mind*:

> A reader of this essay may feel that the outcome is too negative. The three most plausible theories (mind-body dualism, mind-brain monism, behaviourism) are all rejected, and nothing is set forth as the true theory. I readily admit that this essay is only a drop in the bucket. It will serve its purpose if it leads the reader into the writings of Wittgenstein, who is easily the most important figure in the philosophy of mind. It should not be expected, however, that the reflections and observations of his *Philosophical Investigations* or his *Zettel* will somehow add up to another theory. To use his metaphor, philosophical work of the right sort merely unties knots in our understanding. The result is not a theory but simply – no knots![18]

When the philosopher of religion unties the knots caused by a conception of atheism as a theoretical enterprise which demonstrates the illusions of religion, and a conception of theism as a theoretical enterprise to give that same religion a rational foundation, he does not offer either the atheist or the theist an alternative theory, but simply no knots. Yet, when the knots *are* untied, the connections between the language of faith and various aspects of human life remain a theological and not a philosophical enterprise. The theologian is not the only one who may provide religious answers in such contexts. Saints or reformers have their answers too. Nevertheless, in so far as the answer does come from theology, the theologian is a servant of the faith, a citizen of that community of believers who seek a city whose builder and maker is God. Of the philosopher, on the other hand, it must be said, with Wittgenstein, that 'The philosopher is not a citizen of any community of ideas. That is what makes him into a philosopher'.[19]

Notes and References

PREFACE

1. In a collection of essays on philosophy, literature and cultural change, which I regard as a companion to the present book, I have tried to show how literature can provide powerful reminders (not examples) of the ways in which philosophical theories have misunderstood and misrepresented how modes of thought, ways of thinking, can be eroded and lose their hold on people. See *Through a Darkening Glass* (Basil Blackwell and University of Notre Dame Press, 1982).

CHAPTER 1: WITTGENSTEIN AND RELIGION: FASHIONABLE CRITICISMS

1. Anthony Kenny, 'In Defence of God', *The Times Literary Supplement*, 7 February 1975, p. 145. The title is the supplement's, not Kenny's.
2. Rush Rhees, 'Wittgenstein's View of Ethics' in *Discussions of Wittgenstein* (London: Routledge and Kegan Paul, 1970).
3. Anthony Kenny, *Wittgenstein* (Harmondsworth: Allen Lane, Penguin Press, 1973) pp. 229–30.
4. Anthony Kenny, *The Five Ways* (London: Routledge and Kegan Paul, 1969) p. 4.
5. See Kai Nielsen, 'Wittgensteinian Fideism', *Philosophy*, vol. 42, (1967).
6. For further references, see Bibliography, section C.
7. I am described as a 'leading fideist' by Robert Herbert in *Paradox and Identity in Theology* (Ithaca and London: Cornell University Press, 1979) p. 13, and as the arch-Wittgensteinian fideist by Kai Nielsen in *An Introduction to the Philosophy of Religion* (London: Macmillan, 1982) p. 56. According to Nielsen, *The Concept of Prayer, Faith and Philosophical Enquiry* and *Death and Immortality* give 'a detailed paradigmatic statement of Wittgensteinian Fideism' (*An Introduction to the Philosophy of Religion*, p. 200).
8. I am confident that similar evidence could be found in the writings of O. K. Bouwsma, M. O'C. Drury, R. F. Holland,

Norman Malcolm, Rush Rhees, Peter Winch and others. See Bibliography, section B.

9. John Hick, 'Sceptics and Believers', in John Hick (ed.), *Faith and the Philosophers* (London: Macmillan, 1964) pp. 239–40.
10. Walford Gealy, 'Ffaith a Ffydd', (Fact and Faith) *Efrydiau Athronyddol* (1977). It ought to be said that since writing the article Gealy has accepted the force of my textual refutations. He no longer thinks that I have ever held the thesis that religious belief is cut off from other aspects of human life, but he continues to disagree about the *character* of the connections between religious belief and other aspects of human life.
11. Ibid., p. 19.
12. Ludwig Wittgenstein, *Philosophical Investigations*, trans. G. E. M. Anscombe (Oxford: Basil Blackwell, 1953) I, 66.
13. Ibid., I, 65.
14. D. Z. Phillips, *Faith and Philosophical Enquiry* (London: Routledge and Kegan Paul, 1970) p. 78.
15. 'Postscript' in Stuart C. Brown (ed.), *Reason and Religion* (Ithaca and London: Cornell University Press, 1977) p. 139.
16. Ibid., p. 138.
17. D. Z. Phillips, *The Concept of Prayer* (London: Routledge and Kegan Paul, 1965) p. 40 (Issued as a paperback, Oxford: Basil Blackwell; New York: Seabury Press, 1981).
18. H. E. Fosdick, *The Meaning of Prayer* (London: SCM Press, 1915) p. 12.
19. Phillips, *The Concept of Prayer*, p. 116.
20. Dietrich Bonhoeffer, *Letters and Papers from Prison* (London: Fontana Books, 1959) p. 67.
21. Ernest Hemingway, *A Farewell to Arms* (Harmondsworth: Penguin Books, 1960) ch. 9, p. 47.
22. 'Faith, Scepticism and Religious Understanding' (1967) reprinted in Phillips, *Faith and Philosophical Enquiry*, p. 21.
23. 'Religion and Epistemology: Some Contemporary Confusions' (1966) reprinted in Phillips, *Faith and Philosophical Enquiry*, p. 143.
24. Bryan Magee (ed.), *Modern British Philosophy* (London: Paladin, 1973) p. 214.
25. 'God and Ought' (1966) reprinted in Phillips, *Faith and Philosophical Enquiry*, p. 230. Italics added.
26. D. Z. Phillips, *Religion Without Explanation* (Oxford: Basil

Blackwell, 1976) ch. 11, 'Religion, Understanding and Philosophical Method', p. 189.
27. Kai Nielsen, *Contemporary Critiques of Religion* (London: Macmillan, 1971) p. 96.
28. F. C. Coplestone, *Religion and Philosophy* (London: Gill and Macmillan, 1974) p. viii.
29. 'Religious Belief and Philosophical Enquiry', reprinted in Phillips, *Faith and Philosophical Enquiry*, p. 72.
30. T. H. McPherson, 'Religion as the Inexpressible', in A. G. N. Flew and A. MacIntyre (eds), *New Essays in Philosophical Theology* (London: SCM Press, 1955) p. 142.
31. J. A. Passmore, 'Christianity and Positivism', *Australasian Journal of Philosophy* (1957) p. 128.
32. I make such accusations at length in ch. 4 of this book.
33. See D. Z. Phillips, *Death and Immortality* (London: Macmillan, 1970).
34. 'Religious Beliefs and Language-Games' (1970) reprinted in Phillips, *Faith and Philosophical Enquiry*, pp. 92–9.
35. Ibid., p. 108.
36. Coplestone, *Religion and Philosophy*, p. viii.
37. Kenny, 'In Defence of God'.
38. This theme is explored further in ch. 5 of this essay.
39. 'Belief and Loss of Belief' (with J. R. Jones) reprinted in Phillips, *Faith and Philosophical Enquiry*, pp. 116–20.

CHAPTER 2: KNOWING WHERE TO STOP

1. Ludwig Wittgenstein, *Zettel*, trans. G. E. M. Anscombe (Oxford: Basil Blackwell, 1967) 314.
2. Ludwig Wittgenstein, *On Certainty*, trans. Denis Paul and G. E. M. Anscombe (Oxford: Basil Blackwell, 1969) 609.
3. Ibid., 609.
4. Ludwig Wittgenstein, *Philosophical Investigations*, trans. G. E. M. Anscombe (Oxford: Basil Blackwell, 1953) I, 65.
5. H. O. Mounce, 'Understanding a Primitive Society', *Philosophy*, vol. 48 (1973) p. 349.
6. Ibid.
7. Anthony Kenny, 'In Defence of God', *The Times Literary Supplement*, 7 February 1975, p. 145.
8. Richard H. Bell, 'Wittgenstein and Descriptive Theology', *Religious Studies*, vol. 5 (1969) p. 6.

9. Ibid.
10. Ibid., p. 13.
11. Mounce, 'Understanding a Primitive Society', pp. 350–1.
12. Ibid., p. 350.
13. See Wittgenstein, *Philosophical Investigations* I, 23.
14. Ibid.
15. See D. Z. Phillips, *The Concept of Prayer* (London: Routledge and Kegan Paul, 1965. Paperback edn, Oxford: Basil Blackwell; New York: Seabury Press, 1981).
16. For a perceptive statement and treatment of these problems, see Rush Rhees, 'Wittgenstein's Builders', *Proceedings of the Aristotelian Society* (1959–60) reprinted in Rush Rhees, *Discussions of Wittgenstein* (London: Routledge and Kegan Paul, 1970). I have also benefited from a discussion with Norman Malcolm on questions concerning these issues.
17. As we saw, this was one of the theses attributed to philosophers of religion influenced by Wittgenstein. I am indebted in the remainder of this section to a discussion with Rush Rhees, which is not to say that he would necessarily agree with what I say here. See also Rush Rhees, 'Wittgenstein on Language and Ritual' in Brian McGuiness (ed.) *Wittgenstein and His Times* (Oxford: Basil Blackwell, 1982). Rhees' paper is a conclusive refutation of John Cook's claim that Wittgenstein has an *a priori* theory by which all forms of magic and religion are defended from all charges of confusion. See John Cook, 'Magic, Witchcraft and Science', *Philosophical Investigations*, vol. 6 (1983) no. 1.
18. Ludwig Wittgenstein, 'Remarks on Frazer's *The Golden Bough*', trans. A. C. Miles and Rush Rhees, *Human World* (May 1971) no. 3, p. 31.
19. Ibid., p. 19 (quoted in the Introductory Note by Rush Rhees).
20. Wittgenstein, *Zettel*, 22.
21. Ibid., 164.
22. Ibid., 160.
23. Rhees put this forward in discussion simply as a suggestion of how Wittgenstein *might* have made the connection. On the other hand, he insisted that one could not rule out the possibility of this being rejected out of hand by Wittgenstein. In *Religion Without Explanation* (Oxford: Basil Blackwell, 1976) ch. 7, I was puzzled by the analogy between magic and metaphysics. There, however, I was attacking an attempt to

identify them in general, an attempt which is part of a strategy to show that religion is the product of confusion.

24. Rhees, 'Wittgenstein on Language and Ritual', pp. 81–2.
25. *The Interpreter's Bible*, vol. II (New York: 1953) pp. 82–4.
26. Again, this is simply a suggestion as to how Wittgenstein might have developed the analogy.
27. John Passmore, *A Hundred Years of Philosophy* (Harmondsworth: Pelican Books, 1968) ch. 18: 'Wittgenstein and Ordinary Language', p. 450.
28. This is the essence of my disagreement with Mounce's paper which, nevertheless, does stress that religious beliefs, though not mistakes, may be confused, since not all confusion (including metaphysical confusion) can be called mistakes. Mounce would also assign to the realm of confusion, I believe, too many examples of religious and magical practices, which, I would argue, express various possibilities of meaning.
29. For a more detailed discussion, see my paper, 'Religious Beliefs and Language-games' in Phillips, *Faith and Philosophical Enquiry* (London: Routledge and Kegan Paul, 1970).
30. Ludwig Wittgenstein, 'Lecture on Ethics', *Philosophical Review* (1965) pp. 15–16.
31. Rhees, Introductory Note to Wittgenstein's 'Remarks on Frazer's *The Golden Bough*', pp. 27–8.
32. M. O'C. Drury, *The Danger of Words* (London: Routledge and Kegan Paul, 1973) pp. x–xi.
33. Wittgenstein, 'Remarks on Frazer's *The Golden Bough*', p. 31.
34. G. K. Chesterton, *The Everlasting Man*, Apollo edn (New York: Dodd, Mead and Co., 1953) pp. 110–11.
35. Edwyn Bevan, *Symbolism and Belief* (London: Fontana Library of Theology and Philosophy, 1962) p. 11.
36. Ibid., p. 25.
37. Ibid., pp. 26–7.
38. Contrast with the following: 'In the *Iliad* the gods are represented as living on Mount Olympus – on the summit of an actual physical mountain whose lower slopes are familiar and easily accessible to Homer and his hearers. In the *Odyssey*, which is later – and perhaps belongs to a time when Mount Olympus had been climbed and found to be inhabited not by Zeus but only by his eagles – the Olympus of the gods is placed in the sky above all mountains' [Renford Bambrough, *Reason,*

Truth and God (London: Macmillan, 1969) p. 50]. Classicists I have spoken to insist that even in the *Iliad* there is an internal connection between Olympus and the abode of the gods. One does not *first* have the conception of the mountain and *then* discover there are gods on it. On the contrary, Olympus (cf. the heavens) is the high place, the dwelling place of the gods. This does not mean, as I have pointed out above, that climbing a mountain could not affect this conception. [Cf. Peter Winch, 'Meaning and Religious Language' in Stuart C. Brown (ed.), *Reason and Religion* (Ithaca and London: Cornell University Press, 1977) p. 19f.]

39. Wittgenstein, *On Certainty*, 612.
40. Wittgenstein, *Philosophical Investigations*, I, 23.
41. See J. R. Jones and D. Z. Phillips, 'Belief and Loss of Belief' in *Faith and Philosophical Enquiry*, and the final chapter of Phillips, *Religion Without Explanation*.
42. I am grateful to Gordon Graham for urging me to express the point in this stronger form.

CHAPTER 3: REMINDERS OF WHAT WE KNOW?

1. Anthony Kenny, *Wittgenstein* (Harmondsworth: Allen Lane, Penguin Press, 1973) pp. 229–30.
2. O. K. Bouwsma, 'Notes on "The Monstrous Illusion"', *Perkins Journal*, vol. XXIV (Spring 1971) p. 12.
3. Ibid.
4. Ibid.
5. Søren Kierkegaard, *On Authority and Revelation: The Book on Adler, or a Cycle of Ethico-Religious Essays*, trans. Walter Lowrie, (New York: Princeton University Press, 1955).
6. Stanley Cavell, 'Kierkegaard's *On Authority and Revelation*' in *Must We Mean What We Say?* (Cambridge University Press, 1976) p. 167.
7. Joe R. Jones, 'Authority and Revelation in Kierkegaard', *Journal of Religion*, vol. 57 (July 1977) no. 3.
8. Ibid., pp. 234–5.
9. Cavell, 'Kierkegaard's *On Authority and Revelation*', p. 166.
10. Kierkegaard, *On Authority and Revelation*, p. xvi.
11. I owe these points to Stanley Cavell's *The Claim of Reason* (Oxford University Press, 1979) p. 19.

12. Stanley Cavell, 'Ending the Waiting Game' in *Must We Mean What We Say?* p. 152.
13. Ludwig Wittgenstein, *Philosophical Investigations* (Oxford: Basil Blackwell, 1953) I, 124.
14. Cavell, *Must We Mean What We Say?* p. 57.
15. For an alternative translation, see Ludwig Wittgenstein, *Culture and Value*, trans. Peter Winch, (Oxford: Basil Blackwell, 1980) p. 27e.
16. Peter Winch, 'Understanding a Primitive Society', in *Ethics and Action* (London: Routledge and Kegan Paul, 1972).
17. See Peter Winch, 'Language, Belief and Relativism' in H. D. Lewis (ed.), *Contemporary British Philosophy*, fourth series (London: Allen and Unwin, 1976).
18. See p. 34.
19. G. K. Chesterton, *The Everlasting Man*, Apollo edn (New York: Dodd, Mead and Co., 1953) p. 112.
20. Ludwig Wittgenstein, in Cyril Barrett (ed.), *Lectures and Conversations on Aesthetics, Psychology and Religious Belief* (Oxford: Basil Blackwell, 1966) p. 63.
21. Chesterton, *The Everlasting Man*, p. xxii.
22. Ibid., pp. xi–xii.
23. Ibid., p. xvii.

CHAPTER 4: THE CHALLENGE OF WHAT WE KNOW: THE PROBLEM OF EVIL

1. Joe R. Jones, 'Authority and Revelation in Kierkegaard', *Journal of Religion*, vol. 57, (July 1977) no. 3.
2. ch. 1, p. 13.
3. Ibid.
4. Søren Kierkegaard, *Purity of Heart*, trans. Douglas Steere (New York: Harper Torchbooks, 1956) p. 54.
5. Richard Swinburne, 'The Problem of Evil' in Stuart C. Brown (ed.), *Reason and Religion* (Ithaca and London: Cornell University Press, 1977).
6. Ibid., p. 85.
7. This suggestion was put to me by Joseph L. Cowan.
8. Swinburne, 'The Problem of Evil', p. 95.
9. Ibid., p. 84.
10. Ibid., p. 85.
11. Ibid., p. 96.

12. This possibility was put to me in discussion by Renford Bambrough.
13. I am indebted to Peter Winch in the discussion referred to above for suggesting that the unintelligibility lies in this direction.
14. Swinburne, 'The Problem of Evil', p. 84.
15. Ibid., p. 87.
16. Ibid., p. 82.
17. Ibid., pp. 87–8.
18. W. Somerset Maugham, *The Summing Up* (Harmondsworth: Penguin Books, 1971) pp. 173–4.
19. Swinburne, 'The Problem of Evil', p. 89.
20. Ibid.
21. Ibid.
22. Ibid., pp. 89–90.
23. Ibid., pp. 90–1.
24. Ibid., p. 97.
25. Thomas Mann, *The Magic Mountain*, trans. H. T. Lowe-Porter (Harmondsworth: Penguin Books, 1962) pp. 98–100.
26. Maugham, *The Summing Up*, pp. 44–5.
27. Swinburne, 'The Problem of Evil', p. 92.
28. This would be involved in Wittgenstein's notion of putting an end to all the chatter about ethics which we discussed in ch. 2, 'Knowing Where to Stop'.
29. Swinburne, 'The Problem of Evil', p. 100f.
30. Ibid., p. 96–7.
31. Søren Kierkegaard, *Purity of Heart*, p. 72.
32. Swinburne recognises this when he supports my criticism of Peter Geach's appeal to divine power as a justification for obeying God's commands. See R. G. Swinburne, *The Coherence of Theism* (Oxford: Clarendon Press, 1977) p. 205.
33. Swinburne, 'The Problem of Evil' p. 98.
34. Ibid., p. 100.
35. Billie Holiday (with William Dufty), *Lady Sings the Blues*, Abacus edn (Tunbridge Wells: 1975) pp. 183–4.
36. Ibid., p. 187.
37. *Tess of the D'Urbervilles* (London: Macmillan, 1912) pp. 53–4. Quoted in 'Some Limits to Moral Endeavour' in D. Z. Phillips, *Through a Darkening Glass: Philosophy, Literature and Cultural Change* (Oxford: Basil Blackwell; Notre Dame, Indiana: University of Notre Dame Press, 1982).

38. John Hick, 'Remarks' in Brown (ed.), *Reason and Religion*, p. 122.
39. Ibid.
40. Ibid.
41. Ibid.
42. Ibid., p. 124.
43. Ibid.
44. Ibid.
45. For extended treatment of this issue see *The Concept of Prayer* (London: Routledge and Kegan Paul, 1965. Paperback edn, Oxford: Basil Blackwell; New York: Seabury Press, 1981); *Death and Immortality* (Macmillan, 1970) and (with Ilham Dilman) *Sense and Delusion* (London: Routledge and Kegan Paul, 1971).
46. Hardy, *Tess of the D'Urbervilles*, p. 91.
47. Swinburne, 'The Problem of Evil', p. 102.
48. John Wisdom, 'Tolerance', in *Paradox and Discovery* (Oxford: Basil Blackwell, 1965).

CHAPTER 5: BELIEF, CHANGE AND FORMS OF LIFE

1. Ludwig Wittgenstein, *Philosophical Investigations*, trans. G. E. M. Anscombe (Basil Blackwell, 1953) I, 19.
2. This phase in the philosophy of religion is well represented in A. G. N. Flew and A. MacIntyre (eds), *New Essays in Philosophical Theology* (London: SCM Press, 1955).
3. Wittgenstein, *Philosophical Investigations*, I, 66.
4. F. C. S. Schiller, *Problems of Belief* (London: Hodder and Stoughton, 1924) pp. 138–9.
5. J. R. Jones and D. Z. Phillips, 'Belief and Loss of Belief' in D. Z. Phillips, *Faith and Philosophical Enquiry* (London: Routledge and Kegan Paul, 1970) p. 80.
6. See ibid., pp. 79–92.
7. Ludwig Wittgenstein, 'Remarks on Frazer's *The Golden Bough*', trans. A. C. Miles and Rush Rhees, *Human World*, (May 1971) no. 3.
8. Jones and Phillips, 'Belief and Loss of Belief', p. 115.
9. Ibid., p. 116. I say *most* religions because, as Simone Weil points out, there are religions which deify what is dear to many men, namely power and control. These religions she calls

anthropomorphic and naturalistic. See *The Concept of Prayer* (London: Routledge and Kegan Paul, 1965) p. 101f. and p. 158; (paperback edn, Oxford: Basil Blackwell; New York: Seabury Press, 1981). See also my paper, 'On the Christian Concept of Love' in Phillips, *Faith and Philosophical Enquiry*, pp. 247–8.

10. Norman Kemp Smith, 'Is Divine Existence Credible?' in D. Z. Phillips (ed.), *Religion and Understanding* (Oxford: Basil Blackwell, 1967) p. 107f.
11. E. L. Mascall praises A. M. Farrer's remarks in *Finite and Infinite* where he says 'There is no question of demonstrating God from the creatures by a pure inference. God, being a unique existent, must be apprehended if he is to be known at all. But . . . he must be apprehended in the cosmological relation.' Quoted in *Existence and Analogy* (London: Longmans, 1949) p. 69.
12. Norman Malcolm, 'Anselm's Ontological Arguments' in Phillips (ed.), *Religion and Understanding*, p. 61.
13. O. K. Bouwsma, 'Anselm's Argument' in J. Bobik (ed.), *The Nature of Philosophical Inquiry* (Notre Dame, Indiana: University of Notre Dame Press, 1970).
14. J. L. Stocks, 'Desire and Affection' in J. L. Stocks, *Morality and Purpose*, edited and with an introduction by D. Z. Phillips (London: Routledge and Kegan Paul, 1969) p. 40.
15. I have explored some of the relations between philosophical analysis and conceptual change in 'Philosophers, Religion and Conceptual change' in J. Farlow-King (ed.), *The Challenge of Religion Today* Canadian Contemporary Philosophy Series (New York: Science History Publications, 1976) pp. 190–200.
16. I owe this example to Frank Cioffi.
17. See also Phillips, *The Concept of Prayer*, ch. 5.
18. See Simone Weil, *Waiting on God*, trans. Emma Craufurd (London: Fontana Books, 1959) and *Gravity and Grace*, trans. Emma Craufurd (London: Routledge and Kegan Paul, 1952).
19. Elie Wiesel, *Night*, trans. Stella Rodway, in *Night, Dawn, The Accident* (London: Robson Books, 1974) pp. 71–2.
20. See Ian Robinson, 'Religious English' in *The Survival of English* (Cambridge University Press, 1973).
21. Samuel Beckett, *Krapp's Last Tape* (London: Faber, 1959) p. 19.

22. Ibid., p. 20.
23. Ibid.

CHAPTER 6: CAN THERE BE A CHRISTIAN PHILOSOPHY?

1. Ludwig Wittgenstein, *Philosophical Investigations*, trans. G. E. M. Anscombe (Oxford: Basil Blackwell, 1953) I, 23.
2. William Wordsworth, *Poetical Works*, Thomas Hutchinson (ed.), revised by Ernest de Selincourt (Oxford University Press paperback, 1975) p. 522.
3. I am grateful to Norman Malcolm in a discussion of an earlier version of ch. 5 at King's College, London, for emphasising these considerations.
4. Cf. my study of Beckett, 'Meaning, Memory and Longing' in *Through a Darkening Glass* (Oxford: Basil Blackwell; Notre Dame, Indiana: University of Notre Dame Press, 1982).
5. Students at the Perkins School of Theology at Dallas wanted to ask such questions of me and were disappointed when I said I had no answers.
6. Charles M. Wood, 'The Aim of Christian Theology', *Perkins Journal*, vol. XXXI, (Spring 1978) no. 3.
7. Wittgenstein, *Philosophical Investigations*, I, 373.
8. Wood, 'The Aim of Christian Theology', p. 22.
9. Ibid., p. 24.
10. Ibid., p. 25.
11. Ibid.
12. Ibid., p. 26.
13. Ibid.
14. Cf. my paper 'Philosophy, Theology and the Reality of God' in Phillips, *Faith and Philosophical Enquiry* (London: Routledge and Kegan Paul, 1970).
15. Wood, 'The Aim of Christian Theology', p. 28.
16. Ibid., p. 27.
17. Ibid.
18. Norman Malcolm, *Problems of Mind* (London: Allen and Unwin, 1976) p. xi.
19. Ludwig Wittgenstein, *Zettel*, trans. G. E. M. Anscombe (Oxford: Basil Blackwell, 1967) 455.

Bibliography

A. WORKS BY WITTGENSTEIN CITED IN THE TEXT

Philosophical Investigations, G. E. M. Anscombe and Rush Rhees (eds), trans. G. E. M. Anscombe (Oxford: Basil Blackwell, 1953).

Zettel, G. E. M. Anscombe and G. H. von Wright (eds), (Oxford: Basil Blackwell, 1967).

On Certainty, G. E. M. Anscombe and G. H. von Wright (eds), trans. Denis Paul and G. E. M. Anscombe (Oxford: Basil Blackwell, 1969).

Lectures and Conversations on Aesthetics, Psychology and Religious Belief, Cyril Barrett (ed.) (Oxford: Basil Blackwell, 1966).

'Remarks on Frazer's *The Golden Bough*', trans. A. C. Miles and Rush Rhees, *Human World* (May 1971) no. 3.

'Lecture on Ethics', *Philosophical Review* (1965).

Culture and Value, G. H. von Wright (ed.) in collaboration with Heikki Nyman, trans. Peter Winch (Oxford: Basil Blackwell, 1980).

B. SOME WORKS INFLUENCED BY WITTGENSTEIN IN THE PHILOSOPHY OF RELIGION

Bouwsma, O. K., 'Anselm's Argument' in J. Bobik (ed.), *The Nature of Philosophical Inquiry* (Notre Dame, Indiana: University of Notre Dame Press, 1970).

——, 'Notes on "The Monstrous Illusion" ', *Perkins Journal*, vol. XXIV (Spring 1971).

Cavell, Stanley, 'Ending the Waiting Game: A Reading of Beckett's *Endgame*' and 'Kierkegaard's *On Authority and Revelation*' in *Must We Mean What We Say?* (Cambridge University Press, 1976).

Drury, M. O'C., Preface and 'Madness and Religion' in *The Danger of Words* (London: Routledge and Kegan Paul, 1973).

Holland, R. F., 'The Miraculous', 'For Ever?' and 'On the Form of "The Problem of Evil"' in *Against Empiricism* (Oxford: Basil Blackwell, 1980).

Jones, Joe R., 'Authority and Revelation in Kierkegaard', *Journal of Religion*, vol. 57 (1977) no. 3.

Jones, J. R. (with D. Z. Phillips), 'Belief and Loss of Belief' in D. Z. Phillips, *Faith and Philosophical Enquiry* (London: Routledge and Kegan Paul, 1970).

Keightley, Alan, *Wittgenstein, Grammar and God* (London: Epworth Press, 1976).

Malcolm, Norman, 'Anselm's Ontological Arguments' in D. Z. Phillips (ed.), *Religion and Understanding* (Oxford: Basil Blackwell, 1967).

——, 'Is it a Religious Belief that "God Exists"?' in J. Hick (ed.), *Faith and the Philosophers* (London: Macmillan, 1964).

——, 'The Groundlessness of Belief' in *Thought and Knowledge* (Ithaca and London: Cornell University Press, 1977).

Phillips, D. Z., *The Concept of Prayer* (London: Routledge and Kegan Paul, 1965. Paperback edn, Oxford: Basil Blackwell; New York: Seabury Press, 1981).

——, *Faith and Philosophical Enquiry* (London: Routledge and Kegan Paul, 1970).

——, *Death and Immortality* (London: Macmillan, 1970).

——, 'Philosophers, Religion and Conceptual Change' in J. Farlow-King (ed.), *The Challenge of Religion Today*, Canadian Contemporary Philosophy Series (New York: Science History Publications, 1976).

——, *Religion Without Explanation* (Oxford: Basil Blackwell, 1976).

——, *Dramau Gwenlyn Parry* (Caernarvon: Pantycelyn Press, 1982).

——, *Through a Darkening Glass* (Oxford: Basil Blackwell; Notre Dame, Indiana: University of Notre Dame Press, 1982).

Rhees, Rush, 'Natural Theology', 'On Where Does the World Come From?' and 'Religion and Language' in *Without Answers* (London: Routledge and Kegan Paul, 1970).
——, Introductory Note to 'Wittgenstein's Remarks on Frazer's *The Golden Bough*', *Human World* (May 1971) no. 3.
——, 'Wittgenstein on Language and Ritual' in Brian McGuiness (ed.), *Wittgenstein and His Times* (Oxford: Basil Blackwell, 1982).
Winch, Peter, 'Understanding a Primitive Society', 'Can a Good Man Be Harmed?' and 'Ethical Reward and Punishment' in *Ethics and Action* (London: Routledge and Kegan Paul, 1972).
——, 'Language, Belief and Relativism' in H. D. Lewis (ed.), *Contemporary British Philosophy*, fourth series (London: Allen and Unwin, 1976).
——, 'Meaning and Religious Language' in Stuart C. Brown (ed.), *Reason and Religion* (Ithaca and London: Cornell University Press, 1977).
Wood, Charles, 'The Aim of Christian Theology', *Perkins Journal*, vol. XXXI (1978).

C. SOME CRITICS OF WITTGENSTEIN'S INFLUENCE IN THE PHILOSOPHY OF RELIGION

Bambrough, Renford, Introduction in Stuart C. Brown (ed.), *Reason and Religion* (Ithaca and London: Cornell University Press, 1977).
Brakenhielm, Carl-Reinhold, *How Philosophy Shapes Theories of Religion* (GWK Gleerup, 1975).
Bell, Richard H., 'Wittgenstein and Descriptive Theology', *Religious Studies*, vol. 5 (1969).
Cook, John W., 'Magic, Witchcraft and Science', *Philosophical Investigations*, vol. 6 (1983) no. 1.
Coplestone, F. C., *Religion and Philosophy* (London: Gill and Macmillan, 1974).
Durrant, Michael, 'The Use of "Pictures" in Religious Belief', *Sophia* (July 1971).
Gealy, Walford, 'Ffaith a Ffydd' (Fact and Faith), *Efrydiau Athronyddol* (Cardiff: University of Wales Press, 1977).

Haikola, Lars, *Religion as a Language-Game. A Critical Study with Special Regard to D. Z. Phillips* (GWK Gleerup, 1977).

Hepburn, Ronald, 'From World to God', *Mind*, vol. LXXII (1963).

Herbert, Robert, *Paradox and Identity in Theology* (Ithaca and London: Cornell University Press, 1979).

Hick, John, 'Sceptic and Believers' in J. Hick (ed.), *Faith and the Philosophers* (London: Macmillan, 1964).

——, 'Remarks' in Stuart C. Brown (ed.), *Reason and Religion* (Ithaca and London: Cornell University Press, 1977).

Kenny, Anthony, *The Five Ways* (London: Routledge and Kegan Paul, 1968).

——, 'In Defence of God', *The Times Literary Supplement*, 7 Feb. 1975.

King-Farlow, J., and Christensen, W. N., *Faith and the Life of Reason* (Dordrecht: D. Reidel Pub. Co., 1972).

Laura, R. S., 'Positivism and Philosophy of Religion', *Sophia*, (1972).

Maynell, H., 'Truth, Witchcraft and Professor Winch', *Heythrop Journal* (May 1972).

Mounce, H. O., 'Understanding a Primitive Society', *Philosophy*, vol. 48 (1973).

Nielsen, Kai, 'Wittgensteinian Fideism', *Philosophy*, vol. 42 (1967).

——, *An Introduction to the Philosophy of Religion* (London: Macmillan, 1982).

——, *Contemporary Critiques of Religion* (London: Macmillan, 1971).

——, *Scepticism*, (London: Macmillan, 1973).

Passmore, John A., *A Hundred Years of Philosophy* (Harmondsworth: Pelican Books, 1968).

Richmond, James, 'Religion Without Explanation: D. Z. Phillips and Theology', *Theology* (Jan. 1980).

Sherry, Patrick, *Religion, Truth and Language-Games* (London: Macmillan, 1977).

Smart, Ninian, Discussion in Bryan Magee (ed.), *Modern British Philosophy* (London: Paladin, 1973).

Swinburne, Richard G., 'The Problem of Evil' in Stuart C. Brown (ed.), *Reason and Religion* (Ithaca and London: Cornell University Press, 1977).

Trigg, Roger, *Reason and Commitment* (Cambridge University Press, 1973).

D. OTHER WORKS CITED IN THE TEXT

Bambrough, Renford, *Reason, Truth and God* (London: Macmillan, 1969).

Beckett, Samuel, *Krapp's Last Tape* (London: Faber, 1959).

Bevan, Edwyn, *Symbolism and Belief* (London: Fontana Library of Theology and Philosophy, 1962).

Block, Irving (ed.), *Perspectives on the Philosophy of Wittgenstein* (Oxford: Basil Blackwell, 1981).

Bonhoeffer, Dietrich, *Letters and Papers from Prison* (London: Fontana Books, 1959).

Cavell, Stanley, *The Claim of Reason* (Oxford University Press, 1979).

Chesterton, G. K., *The Everlasting Man*, Apollo edn (New York: Dodd, Mead and Co., 1953).

Crosson, Frederick (ed.), *The Autonomy of Religious Belief* (Notre Dame, Indiana: University of Notre Dame Press, 1981).

Flew, A. G. N., and MacIntyre, A., *New Essays in Philosophical Theology* (London: SCM Press, 1955).

Fosdick, H. E., *The Meaning of Prayer* (London: SCM Press, 1915).

Hardy, Thomas, *Tess of the D'Urbervilles* (London: Macmillan, 1912).

Hemingway, Ernest, *A Farewell to Arms* (Harmondsworth: Penguin Books, 1960).

Holiday, Billie (with William Dufty), *Lady Sings the Blues* (Tunbridge Wells: Abacus edn, 1975).

Huxley, Aldous, *Brave New World* (New York: Harper and Row, 1979).

Kenny, Anthony, *Wittgenstein* (Harmondsworth: Allen Lane, The Penguin Press, 1973).

Kierkegaard, Søren, *On Authority and Revelation: The Book on Adler, or a Cycle of Ethico-Religious Essays*, trans. Walter Lowrie (New York: Princeton University Press, 1955).

——, *Purity of Heart*, trans. Douglas Steere (New York: Harper Torchbooks, 1956).

Malcolm, Norman, *Problems of Mind* (London: Allen and Unwin, 1976).

Mann, Thomas, *The Magic Mountain*, trans. H. T. Lowe-Porter (Harmondsworth: Penguin Books, 1962).

Mascall, E. L., *Existence and Analogy* (London: Longmans, 1949).

Maugham, W. Somerset, *The Summing Up* (Harmondsworth: Penguin Books, 1971).

McPherson, Thomas, 'Religion as the Inexpressible' in A. G. N. Flew and A. MacIntyre (eds), *New Essays in Philosophical Theology* (London: SCM Press, 1955).

Passmore, John A., 'Christianity and Positivism', *Australasian Journal of Philosophy* (1957).

Rhees, Rush, 'Wittgenstein's Builders' in *Discussions of Wittgenstein* (London: Routledge and Kegan Paul, 1970).

Robinson, Ian, 'Religious English' in *The Survival of English* (Cambridge University Press, 1973).

Schiller, F. C. S., *Problems of Belief* (London: Hodder and Stoughton, 1924).

Smith, Norman Kemp, 'Is Divine Existence Credible?' in D. Z. Phillips (ed.), *Religion and Understanding* (Oxford: Basil Blackwell, 1967).

Stocks, J. L., 'Desire and Affection' in J. L. Stocks, *Morality and Purpose*, edited and with an Introduction by D. Z. Phillips (London: Routledge and Kegan Paul, 1969).

Weil, Simone, *Waiting on God*, trans. Emma Craufurd (London: Fontana Books, 1959).

——, *Gravity and Grace*, trans. Emma Craufurd (London: Routledge and Kegan Paul, 1952).

Wiesel, Elie, *Night, Dawn, The Accident*, trans. Stella Rodway (London: Robson Books, 1974).

Wisdom, John, 'Tolerance' in *Paradox and Discovery* (Oxford: Basil Blackwell, 1965).

Wordsworth, William, *Poetical Works*, Thomas Hutchinson (ed.), revised by Ernest de Selincourt (Oxford University Press, paperback edn, 1975).

Index of Names

Index of Subjects